SEIZING OPPORTUNITIES

SEIZING OPPORTUNITIES

The reminiscences of a physician

by

RICHARD GODWIN-AUSTEN

The Memoir Club

First published in 2008 by
The Memoir Club
Arya House
Langley Park
Durham
DH7 9XE

British Library Cataloguing in
Publication Data.
A catalogue record for this book
is available from the
British Library

ISBN: 978-1-84104-180-3

Typeset by TW Typesetting, Plymouth, Devon
Printed by The Cromwell Press Ltd, Trowbridge, Wilts

To Jane and Sally

FAMILY TREE

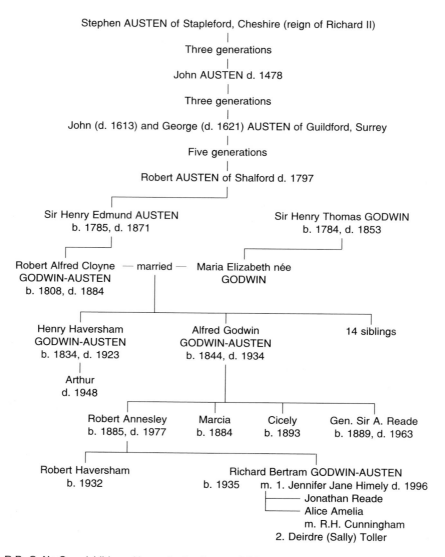

Stephen AUSTEN of Stapleford, Cheshire (reign of Richard II)

Three generations

John AUSTEN d. 1478

Three generations

John (d. 1613) and George (d. 1621) AUSTEN of Guildford, Surrey

Five generations

Robert AUSTEN of Shalford d. 1797

Sir Henry Edmund AUSTEN
b. 1785, d. 1871

Sir Henry Thomas GODWIN
b. 1784, d. 1853

Robert Alfred Cloyne
GODWIN-AUSTEN
b. 1808, d. 1884
— married —
Maria Elizabeth née
GODWIN

Henry Haversham
GODWIN-AUSTEN
b. 1834, d. 1923

Alfred Godwin
GODWIN-AUSTEN
b. 1844, d. 1934

14 siblings

Arthur
d. 1948

Robert Annesley
b. 1885, d. 1977

Marcia
b. 1884

Cicely
b. 1893

Gen. Sir A. Reade
b. 1889, d. 1963

Robert Haversham
b. 1932

Richard Bertram GODWIN-AUSTEN
b. 1935   m. 1. Jennifer Jane Himely d. 1996
├─ Jonathan Reade
└─ Alice Amelia
      m. R.H. Cunningham
2. Deirdre (Sally) Toller

R.B. G-A's Grandchildren: Harry, Annie, George GODWIN-AUSTEN
Rory, Flora-Jane, Jessica Coco CUNNINGHAM

Contents

List of Illustrations

5. General Sir Henry Thomas Godwin KCB
6. Robert Alfred Cloyne Godwin-Austen FRS
7. Maria Elizabeth Godwin-Austen
8. Mount Godwin-Austen (K2)
9. General Sir A. Reade Godwin-Austen KCSI

Prologue

I WOKE EARLY ON THAT BRIGHT June morning and lay contentedly reviewing my situation. Jane was asleep beside me. We had been married so long that there was much we could take for granted. We loved, understood and trusted each other. It was a great partnership that had brought us to a situation where we were both prosperous and respected. We had two children whose lives were progressing happily. My medical career had reached a stage where I could lead my specialist department with the support of my colleagues and of the management. I was confident of my abilities as a doctor, as a teacher, and as a decision-maker in my specialty and profession.

I enjoyed life. It was good to live in a beautiful and historic house. I liked everything in it – from the meticulous restoration of the roof to the well-stocked wine cellar – and I liked the company of friends and the pleasure of entertaining in spacious and rather grand surroundings.

I felt secure. There were no foreseeable financial problems. Of course, I worked long hours and had to set limits to the time I spent on activities such as socialising or gardening but my work brought a sense of accomplishment and competence as well as remuneration. I was secure in my family relationships. I had overcome health problems and could look forward, so I thought, to life continuing in this way for the foreseeable future.

As I lay there relishing these complacent thoughts my mind turned to the events of the day before me. We had been invited out to lunch, with friends we had known since our respective daughters had attended the same school. In those days we were poor whereas these friends were rich, but there was a mutual respect and we always enjoyed their company. Health problems had greatly limited the lives that these friends now led but I was looking forward to a lunch party where there would be much reminiscence and teasing. It was the perfect day for such a party.

We changed for lunch in good time and decided that a dry, sunny day would be a good opportunity to take out the old 1952 vintage

1

Bentley. After all the restoration, this car looked magnificent with its chrome shining, and the dark red and black paintwork.

We had an hour to drive about thirty miles but you couldn't hurry the Bentley and we rolled along comfortably, talking about who was likely to be at the party. The road ahead was straight and I could see my side clear of traffic for nearly half a mile. On the opposite side of the road a line of cars came into view. From the back of this line a blue-green sports car pulled out to overtake the whole line of cars, at increasing speed. I could see that the relative speeds and acceleration would allow the sports car to complete the overtaking in the space available and that there was no need to reduce the speed of my dignified progress. But then, as he was about to pass a yellow van lying second in the line of cars, the van pulled out also to overtake and hit the rear wheel of the sports car. At this point there was some two hundred yards between us. The sports car began to slide and with each correction the skid got worse. He must have had a velocity of eighty or ninety miles per hour. He was skidding sideways down the middle of the road directly towards me. I braked and in the second available steered off the road into a grass verge but there was nowhere to go to avoid collision. Jane said, 'He's going to hit us,' and then there was the bang as the Porsche smashed broadside on to the front of the Bentley. My next memory is turning to see Jane slumped unconscious with blood and swelling on her forehead and blood pouring from her nose and mouth. She did not respond so I opened my door but found I could not put weight on my left knee. I was bleeding from facial injuries and from both legs. Supporting myself on the car I hopped around to Jane's door. She was still deeply unconscious. I checked to see if her neck was broken and unstable and, because she was grey, and I was frightened she would block her airway, decided to lift her out of the car and lie her flat.

So there we were on the grass, she deeply unconscious, gasping for breath, grey but with a neck pulse; and me dripping blood from my face and now unable to stand. A police car arrived but their First Aid box had no relevant medical equipment and the ambulance took twenty minutes to come. They took Jane away immediately. I was given an injection of morphia and left on the roadside to wait for another ambulance – a further ten minutes.

An orthopaedic registrar had seen the crash and with his doctor girlfriend came and spoke to me. Another car driver found the

Bentley bonnet mascot in the grass and put it in my pocket. The person I loved more than anything in the world had been taken away dangerously injured and, I was told later, suffered a cardiac arrest twice on her way to hospital.

When I arrived at the hospital I was already affected with all the optimism that morphia gives. I did not notice the worried faces of the staff involved in Jane's care. It seemed impossible that she was still in danger. I was told that the CT scan of her head was normal. How could she be badly injured with my injuries relatively slight – broken ribs, fractured face bone, ruptured tendon and cuts to my knees? Surely someone would soon tell me the cliché report, 'Her condition is stable and she is showing signs of recovery.' Instead I was told that the chest x-ray was abnormal and urgent angiography would be done to discover if the large blood vessels had ruptured. After four hours of surgery they knew. She had torn the main artery to her right arm on the fractured first rib. There was torrential internal bleeding from the main arteries and back down a vital artery to the brain into the upper chest displacing the airflow to the lungs and compressing other blood vessels.

Suddenly to my horror there was an explanation for everything – the deep unconsciousness, the colour, the gasping for breath and the apprehension of all concerned. I was told that they planned to take her to another hospital where there was a cardiac unit and where her circulation could be supported etc . . . etc.

She was anaesthetised at 8.00 p.m. and closed up at midnight. After by-pass surgery, 40 units of blood and expert work by a team of six they were able to repair the damage.

At about 1 a.m. they came to tell me that she had had several episodes of cardiac arrest. To save her life they had had to tie the major vessels to her right arm and the artery to the right base of the brain, and finally to repair the main artery from her heart. Yes, 'her condition is stable,' but she had a flail chest from rib fractures and 'would need ventilation for several weeks'. I did not dare to ask whether she would survive that long but surely, if I had, the answer would have been 'no'.

From the day after the accident I kept a written record of my thoughts and events. The following is a transcript of this record:

Jonathan and Alice were wonderful. I never saw a red eye. Jonathan supported Alice and they both supported me. What fantastic children.

They transferred Jane back to the hospital where I was, two days after the accident, and I was able to visit her in a wheelchair . . .

> She looked so peaceful in her high bed with tubes everywhere. The children spent most of every day with me. So many friends are praying and praying for her.
>
> On Friday (the fifth day) sedatives were withdrawn but Jane showed only minimal primitive reflex activity and my colleague Dr David Jefferson was realistic when he said that there should be more voluntary response 30 hours after stopping drugs.
>
> The day was spent in prayer with bouts of uncontrollable sobbing. I must not think of myself but think of and talk of Jane. Richard (Alice's husband) was crying like a babe: 'I loved Jane as much as my own mother.'
>
> This experience brings us all closer together . . .
>
> I thought today of her love, her enthusiasm for her family and home, her interest in people and local politics. Her selflessness, generosity and concern.
>
> On Monday 10 June 1996, at ten minutes past midnight they came and told me that Jane was dead. A part of me has gone.
>
> Waves of infinite grief. What a waste of a wonderful person.
>
> Thank you Jane for 35 wonderful years.

Jane had a favourite piece of music that, I think, had come to encompass the meaning of her love. It was the song from *Carousel*:

> 'What's the use of wondrin' . . .'

The last verse starts: 'What's the use of wondrin' if the ending will be bad . . .'

Jane had always insisted that she would die before me and all she would say was that she knew from a certain premonition. Some three years earlier I had been dangerously ill after major heart surgery. Jane had been summoned in the night when my condition had deteriorated. Never once would she allow the possibility of my death to be considered. She prayed, and knew that her prayers would be answered . . . not least because she knew that she would die first.

At that time as I slipped in and out of consciousness I remember her humming,

> 'He's my fella and I love him . . .'

PART 1

The Prime of Life

CHAPTER 1

The ancestors: worthy, industrious explorers

WE ARE TOLD THAT WE ARE ALL the product of heredity and environment, but our genes are determined at random from the pool provided by our parents. Our genetic inheritance is fixed at the time of conception and remains immutable throughout our lives. It is determined as a distillation of a small part of the huge gene pool represented by our ancestors. Family history, therefore, may throw up occasional clues concerning individual personality and character.

The environment on the other hand has an incremental effect throughout life. Experience, relationships, success and tragedy all go to mould the underlying character and personality. In childhood, family and circumstances have a profound effect. At school our contemporaries, probably more than the staff, influence the way we behave and think. Gradually through maturity, experience guides us to follow a particular path. The picture, however, is only complete when the random events and circumstances are added. Illness, bereavement, good fortune and opportunity affect us in unforeseeable ways and how we manage these events often has a profound influence on the rest of our lives.

In these memoirs I have tried to record how possible inherited characteristics combined with the accretion of experience and chance have influenced me.

My family background goes back to sheep farmers in Surrey, who were successful both in producing fine wool and also in marketing it. John and George Austen of Shalford laid the family fortunes in the sixteenth century. George was the squire-farmer, while his brother John travelled as far as Venice to sell the wool. He married Giuliana Grimani, the daughter of the Doge, and her portrait is still in the family collection. John and George Austen collaborated in starting the building of Shalford Park house in 1601 and it was completed in 1611. It was a moderately sized house in late Tudor or early Jacobean style and John Austen died two years after its completion leaving his large estate to his brother and his oldest nephew, John.

John Austen was born in 1590. He was a man who took the responsibilities of his estate and family seriously. He was an uncompromising Parliamentarian and a friend of John Hampden and Cromwell. In the Civil War he served in Onslow's Regiment of Surrey Militia, but hoped, as did Onslow, that eventual compromise might be achieved since the King was as much part of the Constitution as the two Houses of Parliament. I can see many of these character traits in myself as in my immediate forebears.

Three generations spanned the seventeenth century and the sixth squire of Shalford, George, died in 1728. His eldest son John was disinherited in favour of the second son Robert who was another highly respected, worthy and successful man. However he had no children and left all his inheritance to his sister's two sons, 'on condition that they and their heirs . . . on all occasions take and use the surname Austen and bear my Arms.' The Name and Arms of Austen were assumed under the 'Austen Name Act, 33rd of George II'.

Henry, the older nephew, died without issue, but his brother Robert Austen of Shalford had built up a lucrative legal practice at the Bar and on his brother's death moved into and modernised Shalford Park (Colour Plate 2) in the style of Robert Adam. Besides his interest in architecture Robert Austen collected coins and books; and was a connoisseur of art and formed a collection of pictures from the 'Orleans Collection' of Philippe 'Egalite' – the supporter of the 'sans culottes' Revolutionaries. Again we see traits which I may have inherited – see Chapter 10. Sadly his collections were sold when the family fortunes were depleted a hundred years later.

At each generation, there happened to be only one male heir. Thus there were no side-branches to the family tree to dilute the inheritance, and any kindred with Jane Austen must have been earlier than 1500. This changed from the time of Henry Edmund and his successors (see Family Tree, p. vi).

Henry Edmund Austen inherited the family estates in Surrey when he was only twelve years old, on the death of his father, Robert, in 1797. His first marriage gave him nine children of whom Robert Alfred Cloyne was the oldest, born in 1808. Sir Henry Edmund was clearly a worthy and much respected member of the community. He was a JP, supported local good works and charities, and increased the fortunes of the family to a considerable extent. He died in 1871 and it is of interest that a portrait photograph of him survives because photography was still in its infancy at the time of his death (Colour Plate 4).

When Sir Henry Edmund died he was living at Shalford Park, a house he had extended and modernised with the addition of a large bow-fronted drawing room and a seven-bay porticoed entrance façade (see colour illustration p. 2). The house stood close to the church which he rebuilt. The view to the west was across the water meadows of the River Wey towards the ruined abbey of St Catherine's. It was altogether a natural Arcadian landscape much admired in Georgian times.

The funeral of Sir Henry Edmund was a very grand affair, appropriate to his status in the community. The hearse, drawn by plumed black horses, brought the coffin covered with his personal hatchment to the central front door of the entrance façade. It must have made a sight reminiscent of Jane Austen: the abbey in the distance, mist on the water meadows, the neo-Palladian building and the figures in black mourning. My great-grandfather looked out of a window on the scene and was so pleased with the effect that he commanded the funeral procession to 'go round again' so that he could enjoy the scene proceeding round the gravel path in front of the house . . . 'and round again'.

Robert Alfred Cloyne (RAC) carried the name Austen until the double-barrel was granted by Queen Victoria in 1854. The reason for this was following an informal inquiry by Her Majesty.

The story begins with Major General Sir Henry Thomas Godwin KCB (Colour Plate 5) whose only child, Maria Elizabeth, married RAC in about 1833. General Godwin was born in 1784 but his parentage is unrecorded. There is a family fable that he was the illegitimate son of King George III by the royal governess, Jane Gomm, but the evidence for this is obscure and circumstantial. Furthermore, Jane Gomm was only registered as a servant in the royal household some two years after the birth of Henry Godwin. Thus his birth is not registered and the family explanation is that his name and registered parentage was on a page in the register at St Martha's Church, Guildford which was subsequently torn out. However, the register for 1783/84 and '85 are all on the same page, which is complete and makes no mention of Henry Godwin. More convincing might be the fact that a commission in the Army was purchased for young Godwin at the age of fifteen, by an anonymous benefactor (Colour Plate 5). There are, therefore, several intriguing mysteries relating to Godwin's early life.

His subsequent advancement in the Army seems to have been entirely on his own merit and is well recorded. He served in the Peninsular War under Wellington until he was wounded at the Battle of Barossa. Following this he was awarded CB and promoted to the rank of brevet-major. After some years in India he took his regiment into action in the first Burmese War (1824–26). In 1846 he was created Major General and in 1852 he was put in command of the expeditionary force at the start of the second Burmese War. His grandson, Henry Haversham Austen, was appointed as his aide-de-camp in this campaign at the age of eighteen. His most triumphant success in this war was the recapture of the city (and later the province) of Pegu, which led to the annexation of Burma to the British Empire. Godwin's coat of arms had a collar labelled 'PEGU' added to the crest of a lion rampant and this remains on the crest for 'Godwin' to this day. Following the war Godwin returned to India but by that time his health was suffering. He was sixty-eight at the start of the campaign and in spite of his age he was an active and a skilled commander who was described as 'a great favourite of his troops'. Within four months of final victory in Burma, General Godwin died. The notice conveying his KCB and appointment as Colonel of 20th Regiment of Foot arrived after his death and it was his daughter, Maria Elizabeth Austen, who received the honour on her late father's behalf from Queen Victoria. When she went to the palace she was apparently asked by the Queen whether there was any other recognition of H. T. Godwin's services that would please the family. Because Maria Elizabeth was an only child, the name of Godwin had died out on his death, so she requested that her maiden name could be joined to that of her husband so that the family would become 'Godwin-Austen'. This was granted by Royal Letters Patent on 17 October 1854.

The acquisition by the family of a double-barrelled surname affected my grandfather. He had been christened Alfred Godwin but when the surname changed he became Alfred Godwin Godwin-Austen. Thereafter he was always known as 'old Godwin Godwin'.

Robert Alfred Cloyne (RAC) Godwin-Austen (Colour Plate 6) was an amateur scientist. He was also the father of sixteen children by his only wife – the remarkable Maria Elizabeth (Colour Plate 7). His father died when he was sixty-four years old and at a time when RAC had made almost his entire scientific contribution and when his youngest child was sixteen and ready to leave home. He therefore only came to live in the large family house, Shalford Park, when the need for plentiful accommodation was largely past. However, his was a cohesive family, and one where his children and grandchildren (including my father) spent much time visiting each other. The Christmas gathering at Shalford Park must have numbered more than thirty members of the family in 1875.

The sixteen surviving children (she had eighteen pregnancies) of Maria Elizabeth and Robert Alfred Cloyne were remarkably long lived. When the last one died in 1945 the aggregate ages of these children added up to 1,270 years – with two exceeding a hundred, and seven reaching the age of more than eighty-seven.

In the years between his marriage in 1833 and his move to Shalford Park in 1872, RAC had written more than forty scientific papers, he was Secretary and Foreign Secretary of the Geological Society and he was elected a Fellow of the Royal Society. He researched the geology of the south coast of England, the English Channel, and the Channel coast of France. In 1854 he forecast that coal could be mined in Kent and the coalmine in that county only ceased production in 1967. He published textbooks on the Marine Biology of the Northern European Seas and completed the textbook of the Geological Map of England and Wales. At the same time he was caring for his wife who must have been pregnant most of the time (one baby every 16.6 months for 25 years) as well as bringing up his enormous family. It is hard to know which was the greater achievement.

RAC was fortunate to have sufficient means to support his researches and publications as well as his family without having to do paid work. But it still seems somehow creditable that he and all his children made a success of their lives (with the possible exception of my grandfather's extra-marital affair). His portrait drawing was done during his terminal illness but shows him to have been a most handsome man. His wife in her wedding gown looks capable as well as attractive.

Henry Haversham Godwin-Austen FRS

RAC and his children were most influential on my father – especially the oldest son, Henry Haversham ('Haversham'), also Fellow of the Royal Society, the man who discovered the second highest mountain in the world.

When he had been at Sandhurst Military College, Haversham had shown talent in topographical drawing. During his service in Burma as ADC to his grandfather, General Godwin, he developed his skills in surveying and in mapping the creeks and waterways of the Irrawaddy delta.

After Burma he transferred to the Peshawar division of his regiment (The 24th Foot) where he pursued his interest in cartography, survey and watercolour painting. In later life Haversham described meeting General Lord Roberts and making expeditions in to the frontier hills, which had been the scene of the notorious retreat from Kabul fourteen years earlier.

It must have been at this time that Haversham developed an

attachment for 'a good native girl'. He later recorded that she was '. . . not a common woman, of good birth, [her family] landowners in the District of Poonch in the outer hills, not a Kashmiri.'

The product of this affair was a little boy born in March 1857 in Sialkot near Jammu. The child was named Edward. He initially remained in the care of his mother but then was adopted by Mr and Mrs Thomas Milner, a Eurasian couple whose surname he took. This was the time of the Indian Mutiny, but the events in Lucknow and elsewhere appear not to have impinged on regimental life in this part of the Punjab.

At about the time of Edward's adoption, Haversham underwent a Muslim marriage ceremony with the child's mother. How long this marriage survived is uncertain, but in a letter written 65 years later he explained:

> . . . Under strange conditions and very unusual conditions I have always tried to do the best . . . When Mr and Mrs Milner adopted Edward they acted splendidly. I supplied the means (for his education) and they saw him through [so] he got into the Public Works Department and did good work in it. It makes me proud of him . . . I was in the Army on January 1st 1852, in India in 1853 . . . She was a good wife to me and if there is anything now left that I can look back on and love, it is her memory and the way she looked after me.[1]

At about the time he met Edward's mother ('Kudidji') he compiled a map of the Kuram valley. Because this work was considered to be of high quality it was sent to the office of the Surveyor General in Calcutta. As a result Henry Haversham was appointed to the Great Trigonometrical Survey of India working initially in Jammu and Kashmir. However, in the summer of 1857 within months of his son's birth, he was assaulted by some villagers near Jammu. He had to be invalided home to England to recover from his injuries. In 1858 he returned to India and carried out survey work in Budawar and at this time was probably accompanied by Kudidji. There was considerable social stigma attached to the relationship, both by the British military and by Kudidji's family. At the time of the unrest following the Indian mutiny it probably seemed to Haversham that a child of mixed parentage who had seen the horrors suffered by the army at the hands of the Indians would never be accepted in English society. Adoption was the best option.

The end of the affair is uncertain. Kudidji is not referred to after August 1860 and the marriage was probably terminated formally or informally. In the family the story (possibly deriving from what Haversham himself had said) was that Kudidji died and Haversham, released from the marriage, gave Edward into adoption. In 1867 he completed the Karakoram survey. This was a prodigious work, much of it carried out at an altitude of about 18,000 feet. Henry Haversham mapped the greatest glacier system in the world (away from the polar ice caps) and his name remains attached to the highest, the 'Godwin-Austen Glacier'. He discovered and measured the second highest mountain in the world. This mountain had been seen before by Montgomerie from Maramukh in Kashmir about 150 miles away but never surveyed nor its altitude measured. We can visualise this small, tough, energetic and enthusiastic man climbing slowly up the glacier before Alpine mountaineering techniques, let alone equipment, were available. He frequently ascended to above 20,000 feet where availability of oxygen is now considered necessary. Through living in these mountains for several years he was not only tough but acclimatised to altitude.

Henry Haversham was a man of enormous energy and a wide range of skills and interests. He carried out a series of watercolour paintings of the region (Colour Plate 8), and the mountains and glaciers. His painting of the Baltoro and Godwin-Austen glaciers now hangs in the Royal Geographical Society in London. He also had considerable knowledge of geology and he reported to the Royal Geographical and Geological Societies in London the results of his geological investigations. For example, he was the first to describe fossil evidence in the Himalayan foothills and the Siwalik range which established the formation and structure of the Karakoram. Above all, he explored and surveyed K2 (sometimes called Mount Godwin-Austen), its precipitous sides rising two and a half miles at more than 45° to the summit, at 28,287 feet, and first conquered in 1954. He also explored and surveyed the setting of K2 at the head of the Baltoro glacier, which is surrounded within 15 miles by ten of the world's highest peaks.

Haversham made two expeditions to the high Karakoram. On the first in 1860 he was probably recovering from his affair with Kudidji and the birth and adoption of his child. The rigours of his survey work seem to have worked their effect because in 1861 he married Miss Pauline Chichele-Plowden, daughter of a brother officer Arthur Wellesley Chichele-Plowden. One son was born of this marriage

Postage Stamp of India (Mt Godwin-Austin [sic])

(Arthur) but Pauline died in 1871 and Arthur died without children in 1948. There are, therefore, no 'legitimate' direct descendants of Henry Haversham Godwin-Austen; and no legal right through Haversham either to the name Godwin-Austen or to the family inheritance. On the death of Haversham's only child, Arthur (who had no children), my father became the inheritor of the family estates because he was the elder son of the second son.

In 1919 Arthur was 56 years old, married but without children and someone who had always lived in the shadows of his illustrious father and grandfather. His father, Haversham, had another five years to live and was still publishing scientific papers. He had been honoured for his achievements in fields ranging from conchology (study of shells) to ornithology (study of birds) and from exploration to water colour painting. It is hardly surprising that cousin Arthur – who had no achievements to show – was viewed by my father as a failure. Perhaps my father would have liked to be in Arthur's place – the son of the great Haversham. Whether at that time he realised he was likely to inherit we do not know. If he thought of it there was no discernible effect on his ambitions for himself. An incident related by my father may also have influenced him. At about this time Haversham got into debt. At no time had he been remotely interested in money and his second wife, Jessie, was not only extremely beautiful (they married in 1881), but also – so the family suggested – spendthrift and without money of her own. At the bankruptcy hearing the magistrate asked Haversham whether he wished to say anything in mitigation. He reached into a pocket and from a matchbox took out a tiny seashell. 'Your Honour, this shell to me is worth far more than all the money I owe.' He went on to explain why the shell had conchological importance and value.

Certainly this incident must have indicated to my father that if he did inherit one day there was unlikely to be a significant fortune.

CHAPTER 2

My parents: a strangely matched pair

MY FATHER WAS BORN IN May 1885 (and fathered me when he was fifty). He was born the eldest son of parents who lived the life of an Army officer through Imperial Victorian times. My grandfather, Alfred Godwin-Austen ('Old Godwin Godwin') was the second son of Robert Alfred Cloyne Godwin-Austen, and served in the Zulu War in 1878. With the rank of Captain he commanded 'C' Company of the Second Battalion, 24th Regiment when the Regiment landed at East London as part of the Army assembled under Lord Chelmsford for the Zulu War. In July 1878 he led an attack on a group of natives in Natal and was wounded. He was therefore off duty when, on 22 January 1879, the camp at Isandlwana was attacked by Zulus and out of seven hundred white men only about thirty survived. Among the dead was his younger brother, Lieutenant Freddie Godwin-Austen of the Second Battalion 24th Regiment.

My grandfather had a dog called 'Pip' that had accompanied him to South Africa but when he was wounded he gave him to his immediate junior officer Captain Gonville Bromhead, who fought with such distinction (for which he was awarded VC) at the battle of Rorke's Drift. Pip was therefore also at the battle that followed Isandlwana and which lasted all night at Rorke's Drift. Pip was reported to have barked fiercely at any Zulus crawling in the darkness towards the makeshift barricades. The family believe that in addition to the eleven VCs awarded to the defenders of Rorke's Drift surely a twelfth should have been awarded to Pip.

Grandfather Alfred Godwin-Austen was 39 years old when he married Sarah Orred at St George's, Hanover Square on 6 June 1883. He retired from the Army in 1885 with the rank of Lieutenant-Colonel, and settled on the south coast of England to live on his Army pension and to bring up his family. My father's account of his mother draws the picture of a weak and feeble woman. 'Better to give in than give out' (that is 'to die') was her much quoted motto, and to my father it exemplified his mother's inability to take a firm view or decision on anything.

Where Uncle Freddie fell. Isandlwana, S. Africa

Although there can have been little money to spare, a governess was engaged to help with the children. This led to a crisis which was to have profound effects on my father's character, circumstances and development.

When he was about twelve my father was sent to the local private boarding school, St Lawrence College, Ramsgate. His younger brother, Reade, joined him at this school some four years later. In 1900 the four children ranged in age from the oldest (Marcia) at sixteen down to the younger daughter aged seven (Cicely). The governess had been kept on, among other reasons, to look after Cicely. Grandfather at this time had acquired a somewhat racy style, dressing flamboyantly and carrying a silver-topped cane. He enjoyed going to the Music Hall and he must have taken my father many times. The boys much enjoyed singing music hall songs which I was taught fifty years later. 'Knees up, Mother Brown – don't get the breeze-up, Mother Brown': songs which were considered slightly 'vulgar' and therefore at the boundary of what a gentleman would consider acceptable. However, as a child, I found the words incomprehensible.

The social class in which my father grew up would be classified as genteel middle class. There was considerable pride for the family history and antecedents, although increasingly Grandfather appears to have allowed his own standards to slip. As his affections for his weak wife diminished, so he developed a casual relationship with the governess, Annie Bentley.

When he was aged eighteen my father discovered this infidelity and with all the outrage of an adolescent unaware of the ways of the world, decided to leap to his mother's defence. Quite what he expected to achieve it is hard to say. Clearly my father found a *ménage à trois* intolerable and not to be tolerated. There was a major row, which culminated in my father being turned out of the house. His education came to an abrupt end and Grandpa Alfred had no further contact until he attended my parents' wedding three years before he died. It is hard to know what effect the rumpus had on my two aunts and on my Uncle Reade. Each in their own way turned out to be eccentric and wilful but ultimately successful. Whether this was through inherited ability or whether it was from the rigour of having to cope with the collapse of the home and the independence leading from it, it is hard to know.

My father's older sister Marcia he adored. By all accounts she was an attractive, lively person whom everyone loved. However, from her mother she may have inherited some lack of determination and ambition, and from her father a sense of fun and self-indulgence. Clearly she found these characteristics attractive in others as in her thirties she married an impecunious and somewhat wild Irishman. I was given accounts of them travelling with their young son, Gilly, in a horse-drawn gypsy cart along the lanes of Ireland. At this time I suspect Marcia introduced her much younger sister to Ireland and the Irish and this became a passion for Aunt Cicely for the rest of her life. Aunt Cicely had a lesbian lover in Ireland. In my childhood I was unable to understand why Aunt Cicely wore men's clothes – a tie and jodpurs. But this was accepted, and Cicely's gruff voice and butch manner were part of her personality.

Uncle Reade, my father's younger brother, was someone I loved and admired. He was unmarried, but I was told that he had had a

All the Godwin-Austens. From L — self, mother, Aunt Cicely, Robin,
Uncle Reade and father

love when he was young. She was a cousin who had eventually rejected him, and he never found anyone to replace her. Uncle Reade was a career soldier of great distinction. In the second World War he held the rank of Lieutenant-General, under General Ritchie and Auchinleck. I remember discussing with him the campaign in the Western Desert 1940–42. Uncle Reade surprised me in the vehemence of his criticism of Churchill and Montgomery. He explained how Churchill's decision to move forces to Greece in 1941 had extended unnecessarily the war in the desert by two years; and how the replacement of General Cunningham by General Ritchie had led both to the failure of the early campaign against Rommel, and to his own resignation.

Through this resignation the 'Eighth Army lost an able, strong general and a much loved man'.[2] He was awarded the last knighthood KCSI, before Indian independence led to the abolition of the Order.

Marcia's husband, Roland, died of cancer in 1931, leaving Marcia with a small boy. Sadly, she herself died in 1943 when her brothers were preoccupied with the war so that the care of orphan Gilly fell largely to elderly maiden aunts – the relics of the first World War. I, therefore, never knew Marcia but her sweet nature and attractiveness were vividly described to me by my father and by cousin Gilly.

We must return to 1903 with my father still not on speaking terms with his father. However at about this time he obtained an apprenticeship with Francis Beck with a view to achieving a qualification as a surveyor. Francis Beck recurs in this story because it was he who later introduced my parents to each other.

My father qualified as a surveyor in 1906 but found work difficult to come by and without support from his family he decided to emigrate to Canada in 1909. His memories of Canada were somewhat limited by the time he discussed them with me nearly fifty years later but he described the vast emptiness of Canada at that time. In the course of the next four years my father crossed the country travelling 5,000 miles mainly on foot or by river. He worked in any job that he could find but had a fixed idea that he did not wish to live in a town. Throughout his life he always talked of the benefits of 'fresh air' – something that with my scientific training I had difficulty in defining. Certainly Canada in the early years of the twentieth century had little industrial pollution and a great deal of fresh air.

He found work mainly as a logger, firstly in the established provinces of Quebec and Ontario, but gradually moved west through the rebel province of Manitoba and the newly-established states of Saskatchewan and Alberta. His descriptions of life as a lumberjack indicated the extreme hardship of the Canadian winter. The men lived in encampments in the forest relying on provisions they had brought with them supplemented only by supplies largely brought by railway.

I remember his description of making bread in winter when living under canvas and sleeping in a sleeping bag. His problem, he explained, was how to get the yeast to rise before the loaf could be baked. The technique was to make the dough and put it in the bottom of the sleeping bag where through the night with the warmth of your feet, the dough would be ready for baking in the rudimentary oven for breakfast. As children we were intrigued to what extent the feet of unwashed lumberjacks flavoured the loaf.

Although the cold in winter was clearly a threat at all times, in the summer the nuisance of mosquitoes was something that impressed my father. Swarms of mosquitoes would disturb sleep and cause bites which could easily become infected. As a child I had visions of my father covered in mosquito bumps.

This was the time of the Yukon gold rush and although my father was never tempted to join in the prospecting he must have been influenced by the migration of people into the western territories. It is possible that the need to map these territories further developed his interest in survey. When he reached British Columbia, the ownership of land was undetermined over much of the state. It was possible to buy four posts to mark an area of land, register it on a government map and, on payment of stamp duty of 2/6, have your ownership of the land registered with the federal government. This story emerged over the breakfast table in 1948 when my father received a letter explaining he could keep the land he owned only if he took out Canadian citizenship which involved spending thirty days a year in Canada. In spite of attempts by the family to persuade Father to take us to Canada every year, he decided to sell the valuable land he still owned near Vancouver. It probably paid for one term's school fees for my brother and me.

In 1895 the Canadian Pacific Railway had completed the line connecting the east to the west coast. In his travels my father must have met up with workers on the railway. In England he had met and much admired the work of his cousin on the Canadian Pacific Railway. This cousin was to become a lifelong friend and later my godfather.

Bertram Hewitt was the son of Sophia née Godwin-Austen, and a British civil engineer who had earned an impressive reputation as a tunneller. He had been taken on by the Canadian Pacific Railway (CPR) to design the tunnels needed to take the line through the Rocky Mountains. This required a particular form of tunnel curved into a spiral or figure of eight so that within a mountain the track could rise a considerable altitude as well as traversing the mountain. With the very long trains used by the CPR it was possible from the front coach to see the back of the train moving into the tunnel several hundred feet below. Bertram Hewitt's railway tunnels remain one of the remarkable engineering feats of the Canadian railway system. When he completed the job he was given a gold watch suitably inscribed by the CPR, which he left to me in his Will. Sadly the gold watch was stolen in a burglary in 1964.

In the summer of 1914 war broke out in Europe and a huge force of English-Canadian volunteers joined up, including my father.

Recruitment from the French Canadian provinces was relatively small and this led to my father's persisting attitude to the French which amounted to contempt. But in October 1914 my father with 33,000 other volunteers left his beloved British Columbia and crossed back to Europe as the First Canadian Division to fight at the Battle of Ypres. Like so many who endured and survived the horrors of the First World War, my father would rarely talk about it. Within twelve months he had transferred from the Canadian force to the family regiment – The South Wales Borderers (formerly the 24th Regiment of Foot). He was demobilised in 1919 having been commissioned and promoted to the rank of Captain when his younger brother was already a Major and had to be saluted.

He was 34 years old in 1919. He had only his 'demob' pay. He was alienated from his parents but his uncles and aunts were supportive – possibly because they had experiences of my rather wild grandfather's behaviour and admired the stance my father had adopted. In 1919 my father had no fewer than thirteen surviving uncles and aunts. His grandfather (Robert Alfred Cloyne) had died in 1884 and his great-grandfather (Sir Henry Edmund Austen) in 1871. These previous generations and their achievements were something that greatly influenced my father and indeed I myself have great respect for the achievements of the family members in the nineteenth century. He decided therefore to acquire training as a surveyor, inspired by his uncle and his experiences in Canada. He took a correspondence course and returned to a post as assistant to Francis Beck, land agent and surveyor in Buckinghamshire. The Becks had one son, Lionel, who apparently was educationally subnormal. They were relatively elderly and were anxious to find a suitable wife for their son. At school Lionel had been helped and befriended by my mother's brother Norman.

Many years later my mother loved to recount the story. She was invited by the Becks to spend the weekend in the country so that she could be introduced to Lionel. On this weekend she was also introduced to my father who had remained friendly with the Becks. He was 34 years old, she was 18. She fell in love and certainly my father found her coquettish behaviour attractive. At one point, on the tennis court she teased him in such a way that, as she later described it, 'he put me over his knee and spanked me with a hairbrush'. In those days the thought of culpable abuse seems not to have arisen.

Indeed this incident stuck in my mother's mind as a treasured memory for the twelve years that were to elapse before they married.

My father knew that he could not afford to allow a relationship with Beryl Odling to develop and as soon as he had completed training he joined the Colonial Service and was posted abroad.

My mother, Kathleen Beryl Odling, was born in 1901, three weeks after Queen Victoria died. Her father had, as a young man, formed a partnership with two friends to establish a tea-growing business near Darjeeling. One partner provided the capital, the other the business acumen, and my grandfather worked as the tea planter on the estate supervising the work force. It was an extremely successful enterprise. The profits were split three ways between the three partners, and the dividend was paid in November each year. My grandfather working at the eastern end of the Himalayas must have led a somewhat lonely existence, working hard to establish and develop the tea plantation. At the same time my great-uncle was surveying and mountaineering at the western end of the same massif. As far as we know there were no illegitimate family relations in the eastern part of the Indian subcontinent.

After about 25 years working in the tea estate, Grandfather, Arthur Odling, could rely on sufficient income from the business to retire back to England leaving employees to continue the good work. The business survived profitably right through until the 1950s, and provided my mother with an 'AMO dividend' every November which paid for our holidays and school fees.

My grandparents must have married when my grandfather was in his forties. There is little information about my grandmother. I have inherited some furniture that she had, including a small Queen Anne oak cabinet with fitted drawers. This must have stood in the nursery or her bedroom as a child and must have seemed rather plain. My grandmother cut pictures of animals and shells from magazines and stuck them to the front of the drawers and the inside of the doors. The result after 130 years of patina is a delightful and unusually decorative object. My grandmother when on her summer holidays, like all children, collected shells on the beach and these also have gone into the drawers so it has since been known as the 'shell cabinet'.

On their marriage, my grandfather gave his wife a Blüthner piano. He would be happy to know this gave me much pleasure to play and continues to give pleasure to his great-great-grandchildren.

They had four children, three boys and, as an afterthought, my mother. The oldest son, Crawford, was completing his medical studies at the outbreak of World War I so he must have been born in about 1893. Norman and Harold both served in the War. Norman as a young man must have been handsome and good at games. He joined up with a cavalry regiment and was severely wounded in the last cavalry charge in history. His horse was blown up under him and he lost one leg and the use of one arm. He spent the rest of the War in convalescence, and then met 'Bunty', the girl he was to marry. Bunty was my most attractive and charming aunt. She was the daughter of a Church of England missionary to India who had set up a school for Anglo-Indian orphan children. This school, called Dr Graham's Homes, became well-known for the education it provided and the values and discipline it instilled. Dr Graham's Homes still flourishes in Darjeeling and won the annual Christmas charity award organised by a London Sunday newspaper in recent times. Bunty was brought up in Darjeeling where her father and Norman's father had known each other. When Norman had recovered from his trauma and learnt to use the artificial limbs with which he was provided he had to decide what he was capable of doing as a job. Opportunities were limited but in the Depression of the 1920s his prospects seemed bleak. He applied for and was given a job in India at Dr Graham's Homes. He became a trusted director of the school, which he ran when his father-in-law died. His three daughters completed their education in England and every year they organised a bazaar of craft goods made by the children of the school. Many of my Christmas presents came from this source.

Although 'Bunty' seems to us now a name that could come only from the 1920s, Harold, who had also lost a leg in action during the First World War, married someone who was the epitome of that era. Aunt Myrtle had a beautiful round face with huge eyes and long eyelashes. She wore straight, droopy clothes and a small 'cloche' hat. She spoke in the baby voice used by actresses in such shows of that era as *The Boy Friend*. When I knew her she had children several years older than I but she still looked like a flapper from the 1920s. My father had robust views about Aunt Myrtle. He called her a 'flibbertigibbet' and avoided having anything to do with her as much as possible. Curiously my father had two sisters and a wife who never did a paid job in their lives but it was only Aunt Myrtle who came in for criticism as someone who was 'no use to anyone'. When Aunt Myrtle got out her lipstick and powder compact in public my father would go silent and pale.

My mother was born several years after Harold when Grandfather was about fifty years old. Her mother became ill when she was a small child and died probably of tuberculosis when my mother was three years old.

My mother therefore had a most deprived childhood – not in the material sense but deprivation arising from an upbringing by Grandfather's housekeeper; an elderly father who indulged her too much; and brothers who treated their baby sister, not as a playmate but more like a baby doll. They lived at Belsize Square in north London. The boys went to boarding school but my mother grew up looking after her father. The housekeeper, Betty Juby, was my mother's mentor. Their relationship was close and my mother remained in contact with Betty Juby until her death. However, it was a relationship hard to understand from this distance of time. The housekeeper was 'below stairs' and my mother was, *de facto*, the mistress of the house. The gentry were not on familiar terms with the servants in those day, but my mother must have relied on Betty Juby for her education in the facts-of-life in the broadest sense. Apart from Betty Juby (and the two names were always used) the household was exclusively male and this led to a certain tomboyish attitude. It also led to startling ignorance by my mother of some female biology and I'm sure that it was a great relief to her that she had two sons and no daughters to bring up.

My mother grew up through the years of the First World War. She remembered the early part of the war when she was in London. Any man appearing to be old enough to serve but not wearing military uniform would be accosted in the street by an aggressive young woman and given a white feather for cowardice. She remembered the awful news of the constant loss of life at the front, which left her as a young woman with few eligible boyfriends.

It was against this backdrop that her first meeting with my father made such a big impression, while the true purpose of the weekend – to meet Lionel Beck – led to a tragic outcome.

Probably with much encouragement from his parents, Lionel proposed marriage to my mother. This was entirely unexpected by her and of course she rejected him. Two weeks later the unfortunate young man threw himself under a train on the Underground. My mother harboured feelings of guilt over this incident for the rest of her life.

When my father went abroad as a surveyor in the Colonial Service, first to Persia (under the British Mandate) and later to East Africa, he continued to write to my mother and to maintain contact. However, it was not for twelve years that they met again, in England, and he proposed and was accepted.

The twelve years were spent in difficult tropical conditions in the 'bush' of East Africa carrying out survey and cartography. They were very happy years for my father. He was self-sufficient and used to the hard life in encampments. He had no intellectual or artistic interests. He knew little of literature or music. After all, he had had only a truncated education and never lived in civilised society long enough to acquire social skills or intellectual interests, and he had no ambition to do so. He was, however, a great believer in self-education and he contributed to correspondence courses and a subscription to magazines which built up into the *Arthur Mee Encyclopaedia* in eight volumes.

My father enjoyed his work and always emphasised to me how important it was to choose a career that you could enjoy rather than a career with the best financial rewards. He always looked back on his years as a surveyor in Africa with his team of native assistants with great happiness. I never heard him mention the deprivation that such a life must have entailed. Indeed getting married and acquiring new responsibilities at the age of 46 must have been a most stressful event when he said goodbye to the carefree life that he had lived hitherto.

CHAPTER 3

Childhood

I WAS BORN IN October 1935, when my parents were on leave in England. They had married in London in 1931 (All Soul's Langham Place) and my brother, Robin, was born in Tanganyika in 1932 – nine months to the day after their wedding. When I was born my father was aged fifty and throughout my childhood I perceived him as an old man. My mother was sixteen years his junior. In most cases such an age difference would have no significance but in my parents' case part of my mother's appeal was her relative youth in my father's eyes. Indeed it was more than that. My mother would actively adopt a child-like role and baby talk to be attractive to my father. And this behaviour may have been an extension of something she had learnt from childhood with an elderly father and much older brothers. It was behaviour that seemed to me increasingly bizarre as I got older.

My father, like many of his generation, had learnt the importance of 'gentlemanly' behaviour and the value of integrity. Always be 'straight' – meaning honest and considerate – and adopt the leadership role whenever called upon to do so. These were the lessons of my childhood that were instilled into me, and they stuck.

My first memories of my father were of being read to by him before being taken off to bed by my governess, Miss Elliott. I must then have been about four and during that winter we visited my last surviving relative from my grandparents' generation.

Aunt Char (short for Charlotte) was born in 1840 so was 99 in 1939. I remember arriving on her doorstep in afternoon darkness and the maid offering soup, which seemed to me to be most incongruous. Aunt Char was a fearsome sight to a small child because she was bald, huddled in a wheelchair and used an ear trumpet. She died nearly six years later, the last survivor of RAC's sixteen children. Through my contact with Aunt Char I can claim to have met someone who was born in the year that Queen Victoria married Prince Albert and their first child was born.

The year I was born was, by contrast, a year of gathering oppression. Mao Tse Tung completed his 'Long March' in the month

28

Robert Annesley Godwin-Austen CBE

I was born and Hitler had complete control in Germany and was actively re-arming. Stalin's bloody purges of the Communist party were killing thousands and drove Trotsky to flee to Norway. These portents came to fruition in my early childhood.

When I was four we were living in Cyprus where my father was Director of Surveys in the Colonial Service. The outbreak of war seemed to have had little impact until the German invasion and capture of Crete. This led my parents to conclude that an invasion of Cyprus could be imminent and that my older brother and I would be best moved to a safer place outside the war zone. Without any knowledge of South Africa (my father had worked only in East Africa) they formed a plan for Miss Elliott, our governess, to go with their two children to South Africa, leaving my parents in Cyprus to endure and fight in any German invasion of the island. It was an extraordinary plan. It is hard to understand in retrospect how my mother was able to overcome her maternal instincts and allow total responsibility for her children to pass to someone she had employed for barely three years. The decision to leave her husband, however, would have been equally difficult.

In the event, Miss Elliott, Robin and I were put on a ferry to Port Said in Egypt on the first stage of our journey to South Africa. I remember being put to bed in a small hotel in Port Said. It must have been about eleven o'clock at night when I was woken by Miss Elliott and carried down to the basement of the hotel. There I was told that the Germans were dropping bombs on our hotel and on the town. I accepted this information without any sense of fear or anxiety. Much more interesting to me at the time was the fact that the basement was crowded with grown-ups who were behaving in a most peculiar way. I later asked Miss Elliott who told me that they were so frightened that they had all got very drunk!

In retrospect, this episode illustrates a child's reaction to an extraordinarily stressful situation. I had just been taken from my home and from my parents. I was travelling to a strange and distant country. I was experiencing the reality of war, and yet I was not apparently distressed in any way. Instead I simply accepted it all as the natural course of events over which only the grown-ups could exert any control.

Our ship arrived in Durban, South Africa after a few peaceful weeks at sea. The 'refugees' (as we were now called) were taken to the YMCA where volunteers were matching us to accommodation offered by local families who had an unoccupied spare room. The three of us, Miss Elliott aged 39, my brother Robin aged eight and myself aged five were allocated to a couple who lived in a village called 'Kloof'. This was some miles inland from Durban and I suppose that we must have travelled there by train.

It was a large, slightly gloomy old house. I learnt that our host, Mr Cowley, was a barrister defending criminals in Court and I concluded that this was a slightly disreputable job. He dared not interview them in his house so he had built a small hut in the garden where he met his clients. Both Mr and Mrs Cowley were elderly, rather remote but kindly figures. Their care and generosity was remarkable – the more so since South Africa seemed to be so little affected by the war. Indeed if Miss Elliott had not taken a voluntary job making meals in the NAAFI we would probably have forgotten the war was going on. Miss Elliott told me stories of airmen and sailors she had met and one

Robin and self, Kloof, Natal 1941

I remember, David Mahoney, was invited to my sixth birthday party. He was a sailor who had obviously formed some attachment to Miss Elliott.

Looking back I have a great sense of sympathy for Miss Elliott. She came from a Northumbrian family and had been sent to Liverpool to qualify as a nanny. She was of the generation where so many young men had died in the First World War that social life, male friendships and marriage prospects were very limited. Through her 20s and 30s there was the depression and employment was uncertain. She was then overtaken by the events of the second war with the massive responsibility of caring for two young children on her own in a strange country.

Miss Elliott had been brought up in a respectable middle-class family. Her education was very limited, but she had a very practical approach to life. The upbringing she gave encouraged respect and trust, but disciplinary boundaries were clear; there was to be no

Miss Anne Elliott 1941

'sneaking', and obedience at all times was expected. My debt to Miss Elliott was enormous and certainly not discharged by caring for her during her final years. She died in her 99th year having outlived all the friends and relations of her own generation. When she died all her worldly possessions could be fitted into a suitcase.

Robin and I were sent to the local 'Government' school where we encountered the hardy sons of the local Afrikaners. I have fond memories of growing up in this immense, empty country of *veldt* and *kloof*. We climbed trees and we dammed streams and probably led a wild life, which has seemed increasingly Arcadian with the distance of time.

At the end of our time in Africa, probably in 1944, I was sent to a boarding school (Cordwalles) where my brother had been for two years. The shock was mitigated by Miss Elliott taking a job as assistant matron at the school.

The school was a remarkable anachronism. The headmaster was an Old Etonian and had developed the school very much on the lines of what he had learnt at Eton. As a result, Sunday would see the boys trooping into chapel dressed like little Etonians. I was then aged eight and wore short trousers, white shirt, grey jacket and (crowning glory) a hard, starched Eton collar. For those unfamiliar with this shirt accessory, the Eton collar is about two inches wide, hard-starched, and is attached to the shirt with two studs. It is worn outside the lapel of the jacket with a loosely knotted tie. I can remember the panic of struggling to force the studs through the starched apertures in the collar and then tucking the jacket collar under the shirt collar before running to be in time for chapel. We were kept in order by the school monitors – boys who were probably no more than thirteen (but who seemed entirely adult). They were dressed in tailcoats with bow ties. All this traditional fancy dress was worn in tropical temperatures.

While we were in South Africa, my mother, along with all the women and children, was expelled from Cyprus by Government decree. She knew that we were in Natal but war secrecy meant that she did not have our address.

One day, Miss Elliott decided to take us to the barber in Durban. As we came out after the haircut Miss Elliott suddenly exclaimed, 'There she is!' By coincidence my mother as her first task on arrival had gone to the bank, which happened to be next door to the hairdresser. It was the first but not the last extraordinary coincidence in my life.

With my mother's arrival in South Africa, Miss Elliott's role as sole carer of my brother and me became superfluous. Money must have been short. My mother was untrained for any form of employment – even caring for her children – but Miss Elliott was employable and therefore left us to care for another refugee family. She was to look after the children of the Governor of Cyprus, Sir Andrew Wright, whose wife was crippled by severe rheumatoid arthritis. The loss to me of my beloved Miss Elliott, who had been a feature of my life from the age of two or three, must have been most traumatic but curiously I have no recollection of sadness. Once again the 'take life as it comes' reaction of a child seems to have operated and my memories of the remaining time in South Africa are happy with that country always idealised in recollection. Indeed I am a good example of the Jesuit precept – 'Give me a child until he is seven years old and I will have him for life.'

In 1944 my father was able to take leave in South Africa and, with my mother, to arrange the return to Cyprus before travelling on to England. The most exciting part of this journey was the ship from Cyprus to England.

It was December 1944 and enemy submarines were still attacking shipping in the Atlantic. Our journey back to England began with a stay in Haifa in what was then still Palestine. We spent Christmas in Haifa. I was taken to a midnight carol service in a church said to have been built over the cave that had been occupied by Elijah. The church was small with white walls and thick columns with a low domed ceiling and apse. It smelt of incense. I remember the magical experience of hearing a boys' choir singing 'See Amid The Winter's Snow' in flickering candlelight. I was just nine and had only seen snow once when it had been brought to show me in a Thermos flask – from the Troodos Mountains in Cyprus.

After several weeks in Palestine, a ship was able to offer us (mother, brother and me) passage to England. It was a small tramp steamer with everything in welded and riveted steel – the decks, the walls of the small cabin, the bunks and even the shelf for the suitcase with our possessions. We boarded and explored and then watched fascinated as cranes lifted huge packing cases into the hold. The cargo must have been produce for war-stricken Britain but I had no idea of rationing. I had experienced the plenty of South Africa and was about to understand why England was suffering at the basic level of food and clothes rationing.

We sailed quickly through the Mediterranean and as soon as we were through the Straits of Gibraltar, Atlantic storms and high seas hit us. It was extremely cold and for many days we all suffered frightful seasickness.

We seemed to be making very little progress and then my mother noticed we were sailing in circles. How she discovered this I don't know as there was certainly no sun to be seen, only dark grey clouds and a high sea. The explanation was that we were waiting for a protected convoy of ships from America before entering the English Channel where U-boats were still operating south of Ireland. So for about two weeks we circled west of Biscay. By this time I had got over my seasickness and could climb up the steel ladders and slither along the wet steel decks wrapped in every piece of clothing I could muster. Standing on an open deck looking forward I remember the front of the ship pitching into the huge waves with sea swamping over the foredeck and round the raised hatches into the hold. The prow would eventually lift out of the water as the wave passed under us and I could feel the deck tilt and pitch under my feet, and the cold wind and spray whip over my face and through my hair. I cannot believe that I found the experience exhilarating but it was new and at that age there was an insatiable need for the new experience and information. I had already learnt of the physical stress of climbing mountains, so the wind, the cold and the sea were an experience not to be missed.

At this time, my Uncle Reade (General Godwin-Austen) was at the War Office in London. Somehow my parents must have communicated with him because arrangements had been made for us to be met when we finally docked at Tilbury.

It took all day to manoeuvre our ship through the docklands. I had expected as speedy an arrival as our departure from Haifa, but through the afternoon we were still slowly moving deeper into the huge areas of docks that then existed and it was dark before we finally berthed. A large black car with driver from the War Office awaited us on the quayside. We were driven in the blackness of total blackout through the East End to the only address in London that my mother had – 100 Constantine Road, Hampstead. This was the house given to Betty Juby, my grandfather's housekeeper, after she retired.

It was a two storey Victorian terrace house with two rooms on each floor, comfortable for a single old lady but bursting at the seams with the arrival of my mother and two young children. Behind the houses opposite was a school playground and in the middle of the concrete floor was a huge bomb crater caused, I was told, by a V2 rocket. I never had further knowledge of V2s but remember the last of the V1 'doodle bugs' or flying bombs.

My mother's first task was to send my brother and me to school outside London. Her best contact was her brother Harold, who had four sons ranging from late teens to slightly younger than I. Through Harold she wrote to Radley School where his older sons were and Robin was sent away almost immediately. She then made arrangements for me to go to the school where Harold's boys had also been. In the bitterly cold and snow-covered winter of 1945 I found myself back in a boarding school with few similarities to my school in South Africa. Boxgrove School was staffed by men too old to serve in the war. Some showed little indication of any training to be a school teacher, but I received the rudiments of an education – not only a formal introduction to the classics and English literature and history, but also the facts of bullying, childhood covetousness and pederasty. The most intense memories were of sitting on the coke-burning stoves (which were the only source of heat) and shivering with cold. There was also tobogganing instead of games, and ice-skating on the frozen pond. I was quickly aware of the difference from the warmth and plenty of South Africa. After lunch each day we would queue up to be given a ration of two sweets (Mars Bars were cut into six pieces) and then we were read to for half an hour – Buchan, Conan Doyle, Rider Haggard and Rudyard Kipling. So much did I enjoy this that I found the books in the library and spent all my free time curled up in a chair reading my way through the collection.

At the start of my prep school career I was intensely homesick even although I had no home. For the first time I experienced the all-encompassing sense of hopeless misery and despair: the loss of constant support and supervision from a parent and its replacement with a routine where I was expected to take responsibility for being in the right place at the right time with the appropriate books and dressed correctly. Life became a sense of inadequacy and above all without care or friendship from anyone. These feelings passed within about two weeks. They were displaced by friendships within the school – after all, we were all making the same adjustments – and by a state of mind, which constructed two separate worlds – school and home. This construct became distressing at its boundaries – that is, going home or returning to school. At the end of term I remember how anxious I was to leave the school as quickly as possible, ideally without my parents or the car being seen. Similarly visits by parents (representing the home environment) were incongruous and irrelevant at the school – to watch football matches or the like – and I would have been horrified if in the holidays a member of the school staff had visited my home. As long as the two – home and school – could be kept separate I could cope with and learnt to enjoy the company and what I was doing. Friendships were based on shared experience leavened with the spirit of competitiveness. But although my contemporaries were able and civilised, no persisting friendships were developed and I have never met a friend from that time by chance.

When I was just thirteen I moved to Charterhouse. It was decided not to send me to Radley, firstly because my brother claimed that he was unhappy there and also for the less important reason that I preferred games to rowing. On reflection I cannot remember any occasion when my brother admitted to pleasure or enjoyment. I think he had found it was safer to earn the sympathy of parents by always emphasising the worst.

My transferral to public school was almost as stressful as starting prep school. The impersonality of the environment where there was no help or indication of concern brought back the same dread and sense of hopelessness that I had experienced some three years before. But I had learnt how to make friends and I enjoyed the increased sense of freedom that my new school provided. I was a good swimmer and in the summer term I practised swimming daily. This eventually led to a place in the school swimming team, competitions, prizes and, most fun of all, 'away' matches at other public schools.

In those days it was the tradition at Charterhouse to swim naked. In retrospect this tradition seems most bizarre and in the contemporary climate of sexual awareness where nakedness is considered suspect outside the bathroom, it seems to run needless risks in a single sex pubertal community. It is also relevant that pre-war the school had been notorious for homosexual activity, which had created a scandal only overcome by the appointment of a headmaster who imposed ruthless discipline to control the situation. Since leaving Charterhouse I have, of course, been aware of books written by my contemporaries (Frederick Raphael and Simon Raven), books which describe rampant homosexuality. It must be a measure of my naïvety that I was entirely unaware of this at the time – unless these books owe more to the fantasies of the authors than they do to reality! Certainly, swimming naked did not seem to cause any problems beyond the difficulty of having to find a bathing costume for school swimming matches.

Charterhouse has a situation and architecture unequalled by any other public school except perhaps Stowe. But unlike Stowe, Charterhouse was built as a school, and as the school has enlarged and new buildings have become necessary the quality of the architecture has been maintained using the same materials and scale and not least by employing three architects whose designs create a harmonious and coherent architectural landscape. The boys respond to these surroundings almost subconsciously and, looking back, the magic of walking round Green on a summer Sunday evening before chapel is a treasured memory. The setting sun turns the original Hardwick buildings and the Gilbert Scott Memorial Chapel a golden orange standing on the plateau of green playing fields.

For me the achievement of the school was to give every boy the opportunity to develop talents and interests. Class work was rightly emphasised and academic achievement was recognised by the school and rewarded. The staff were motivated and enthusiastic – in contrast to many whom I had met at prep school. The curriculum seemed to have originality built into it so that the teaching of English subjects – literature, history and geography – sparked enthusiasm I had not previously experienced. But the greatest change from my previous schools was the amount of free time available. To begin with, when everything was unfamiliar, the day was made up of hurrying frantically to get from one class to the next or to chapel; alternating with long periods of time when there was nothing specific to do. Gradually one learnt of the huge range of 'clubs' organised by boys or staff. They were always anxious to recruit new arrivals. In this way I was persuaded (at the cost I believe of 2/6) to join the radio club – making your own 'crystal set' or valve radio; the photographic club, where one could use facilities for developing and printing photographs; the poetry club where individuals learnt and recited the verse of their choice and were encouraged to write poetry. This club was popular chiefly, I suspect, because like the 'Music Soc.' it met in a beak's house where a small glass of sherry was offered to those over sixteen.

My parents paid for me to continue with piano lessons. I had started under the disciplined supervision of the kindly old maid at my prep school (Miss Scott). Leonard Halcrow, my music beak at Charterhouse, was very different. He seemed young, talented and easy-going. He was endlessly patient and encouraging. When it was obvious I had had enough music for one day he would fill the lesson with wide-ranging conversation on topics of interest to me. He had a sharp sense of humour and combined this with a sense of tradition and a deep moral sense. I learnt much later that he became Chairman of the Magistrates' Bench and held the position for many years.

Music and painting were much encouraged and both occupied a considerable amount of my time. Ian Fleming Williams was the beak-in-charge of Art School and was the second most important influence on me. He dressed as expected in corduroy jackets and baggy grey flannels with loose woollen ties. Like Halcrow he was enthusiastic and energetic, always ready to find something to praise in one's naïve attempts at painting, sculpture or pottery.

When I was about 16 a friend and I hit on the idea of starting a new 'club'. It was to be – rather pompously – devoted to 'the appreciation of the visual arts'. We discussed this plan with Ian Fleming Williams who typically became very enthusiastic and suggested that we name our club 'The Beerbohm Soc.' – after the eminent Old Carthusian artist and writer. The new club had to find a range of activities which would at the same time attract members, prove enjoyable and promote 'the appreciation of the visual arts' – including the performing arts.

Once again under the influence of Ian Fleming Williams, James Kirkman, my co-founder, and I wrote a series of letters to a whole range of museum curators, art gallery owners and organisers of art exhibitions ending up with an outrageous request to Glyndebourne for reduced price opera tickets for the education of schoolboys about opera. In retrospect I am astonished that we received generous offers of hospitality to our requests, and I have very happy memories of taking a coach of thirty schoolboys to Agnew's in Bond Street where Mr Agnew himself showed us round the exhibition and then gave us all tea and biscuits.

Our greatest triumph, however, was to be allowed to attend the final dress rehearsal at Glyndebourne of *The Seraglio*. Again a coachload of Carthusians was warmly received at 2 p.m. on a Sunday afternoon to watch a spectacular production having paid £1 each for the privilege. Even in 1951 this was a bargain and of course it sparked in many of us a lifelong enthusiasm for opera, art galleries and country houses.

In my last year at Charterhouse I was prevailed upon by contemporaries and by my house tutor to audition for a production of *Romeo and Juliet*. Charterhouse in those days was boys only, so the auditioning process was risky. So it turned out in my case when I was cast in the role of Juliet's nurse. However, after initial dismay I discovered what a wonderful part this is. My closest friends all achieved speaking parts and rehearsals were hugely enjoyable. James Kirkman, already mentioned as my co-founder of the Beerbohm Society, was cast as Peter, the servant to Juliet's nurse.

Juliet's nurse and Peter (James Kirkman) 1953

The production which ran for three nights was a huge success – so much so that the producer and house tutor decided to take the production to Paris where we would perform in front of an audience of French schoolchildren. The costumes had been the responsibility of the wife of a junior master. We were all at a most impressionable age and saw in this lady a fantasy of beauty and sexuality. She was very aware of the effect she had on pubescent young men. She enjoyed playing the role of coquette with vivacity and slightly risqué remarks. Olivia (not her real name) was effectively co–director of the production and as such accompanied us to Paris where she took great pleasure in suggesting outings to Harry's Bar and the Bal Tabarin. This whole episode turned out to be educationally import-ant to me.

At Harry's Bar I was sitting on a high bar stool. After about two drinks – probably gin and orange – I suddenly started to feel extremely dizzy. A moment later I found myself semi-conscious on the floor looking up into a circle of anxious faces.

At the Bal Tabarin cabaret I learnt something of another aspect of adulthood. The Chorus of Nudes was something that I had never previously seen and I learnt the delights of the female figure. And in the company of Olivia I became aware that I could be perceived by others as sexually desirable – surely the most important part of sexual maturation. In this way I learnt to be very careful about the consumption of alcohol and less careful and more adventurous in my approach to women. These were important lessons to be learnt at school – probably as important as many other aspects of my education at Charterhouse.

In my last two years at Charterhouse, the influence of the school regime became increasingly important. More and more we were treated as intelligent, responsible adults and we responded by taking increasing pleasure in achievement. There was the added effect of competition especially in class. We were all encouraged to do better than the boy at the next desk, and the house was treated to special celebrations whenever a boy won a scholarship to University.

I was a poor performer on the games field. Team sports especially failed to enthuse me. In spite of being at Charterhouse in the heyday of such giants as Peter May, I considered cricket to be a game which filled a great deal of time with remarkably little useful activity. Individual (or 'Minor') sports were better and without particular distinction, I played much tennis, squash, rackets and fives. But my favourite sport was swimming. Eventually I achieved a place in the school swimming team and for two summers enjoyed the competitive swimming against other schools.

More liberal encouragement to learn meant that we all worked hard in the sixth form. We were expected to synthesise our learning, and to argue a point. I remember writing essays such as 'The foetus is a parasite on its mother. Discuss' and 'Compare and contrast the structure and function of the skeleton of a dogfish with that of a rabbit'.

Looking back it seems the problem for the master in marking these essays must have been as testing as the task of the student writing them but it was a wonderful education which encouraged original thought, clear expression and reasoned argument. These were all talents that fitted us for the professions most of us were later to take up – in the law, medicine and business; and in the Civil and Foreign

Services. In my own case I had decided I wanted to take up medicine and having failed on my 'A' level results to get a place at Cambridge I applied for and achieved a place at St Thomas's Hospital Medical School where I started in 1953.

CHAPTER 4

Medical student days

I WAS JUST EIGHTEEN WHEN I STARTED my medical studies at St Thomas's Hospital. The NHS had been established barely five years and my teachers were all doctors who had known service in the war and medical practice before the nationalisation of health care. They were unaware that with nationalisation would come an encroaching bureaucracy that would limit and ultimately remove professional independence. At that time the three gentlemen who sat facing me at the interview for a place in Medical School were clearly a Medical Nobility. They expected respect from patients, nursing staff and from the handful of hospital administrators. They dressed, if not in frock coats, always in a suit with a gold watch and usually a starched collar (detached). Everyone was aware of their professional status, defined as the command of specialised knowledge and medical expertise, and a rigorous ethic, which demanded that the first and encompassing duty of the doctor was to his patient. His only other duty was to his profession. No one had even considered that the doctor might have a duty to fulfil a contract of work to the NHS.

Selection for Medical School seemed almost automatic. It is true that I had passed three 'A' level examinations (I do not remember that grades were applied in those days) but the interview apparently determined one's future career. After the event it seemed that it was those who failed to show sufficient respect for the interview panel who failed to get a place in medical school. Some tried to be humorous in their answers, or were so banal in their replies that they seemed unsuitable as doctor material. One candidate when asked why he had applied to St Thomas's Hospital replied that it was only because it was so convenient for Waterloo Station.

My short haircut, blue suit and respectful manner secured my place and with my mother I embarked on the next task of finding 'digs' in London.

I had left Charterhouse at the earliest reasonable opportunity – the decision not uninfluenced by my parents' enthusiasm to be relieved of the burden of school fees. These were a crushing £80 per term and they wanted to avoid incurring heavy expenses on my behalf as a medical student. My medical school fees were paid by a State Scholarship, which was awarded, not on merit, but by the good fortune of my parents living where the local authority was relatively affluent. My digs were another matter and together with a small allowance were the responsibility of my parents. A room in digs with Miss Sheffield seemed suitable from every aspect.

Miss Sheffield was an ageing radiographer who had a small flat in Kensington which was respectable, clean and cheap. Like Miss Elliott she seemed rather severe and proper. I sometimes wondered how she had coped with an earlier lodger, Clement Freud, the Liberal MP, broadcaster and *bon viveur*.

The flat was fairly bleak and the only unusual feature was a small balcony completely filled with dozens of pots of bright red geraniums. These were carefully layered in newspaper in a cupboard through the winter and potted up in the spring. Kensington had a garden competition and Miss Sheffield was wholly committed to winning the 'balcony' section every year.

She was a lonely soul and she made it clear to my mother that she wanted the lodger to take supper most nights – so that there was someone for her to talk to. These suppers were pretty agonising but I would escape to my room immediately after the meal with the excuse that I needed to study my textbooks. Occasionally Miss Sheffield would invite a friend to supper when I would be introduced. The only memorable such occasion was when a large and fearsome friend of Miss Sheffield arrived with her sixteen-year-old daughter, who was extremely pretty. She was wearing a yellow party dress and was shy with downcast eyes, hardly speaking all evening. Her mother had been widowed in the war and had two daughters whom she was anxious to introduce to eligible young men. A few days after the supper party I received an invitation to spend the weekend at their house in Kent. I duly arrived at the station to be met by the mother in an ancient Riley. She asked if I could drive, and when I admitted that I could she demanded that I took the wheel and drove to their house. I was an immature and rather shy individual who found the experience to be unnerving for many understandable reasons. To be asked to drive a car belonging to some one I had only just met made me apprehensive, not least because the gear had to be 'declutched' when changing gear and there was an appalling grinding sound as if the cogs were being stripped from the gearbox and scattered in the road behind us. I expected never to be invited again but, on the contrary, many pressing invitations followed and to avoid serious compromise I had to construct increasingly implausible excuses.

The mother's concern to get her daughters married was unjustified. Both Pegga and Gillian Bird were most attractive and capable girls and Gillian remained a close friend for the rest of her tragically short life.

At the start of medical school I was bought a tweed jacket and a nylon shirt to be washed every night, hung in the bathroom at Miss Sheffield's to 'drip-dry' and to be worn again the next day. These articles of clothing were incredibly robust and I think they lasted me the five years of my medical school career.

To get to the hospital I had to walk from Westminster Underground station over Westminster Bridge and I have blessed memories of the view of St Paul's – 'earth hath not anything to show more fair'. The old 'Nightingale' building of St Thomas's Hospital was also an inspiring sight. We were able to sit and have coffee on the terrace facing the Palace of Westminster and talk, argue and exchange views and experiences. At the age of eighteen friendships are easy and lasting. There is a hunger for opinion on politics, sex and religion. These and many other subjects occupied many happy hours of earnest discussion. I was fortunate to find myself with a group of intelligent, ambitious, like-minded people with the idealism of youth combined with the determination to have a good time. We all smoked and drank quite prodigiously but these practices never seemed to cause detriment to our work. Now, fifty years later, none of my group has suffered illness or death from smoking or drink-related disorders. Not a statistically significant sample but, at the same time, a fact to bear in mind when in the new millennium so much prominence is given to exhortation against smoking and alcohol. Few of us took significant exercise. Jogging was unheard of and the facilities for sport were limited and inconvenient. Likewise we were uncreative and even those who had become competent on the violin or piano at school tended to give it up and concentrate on their studies. It is not surprising that in universities at that time the medical students were regarded as a rather boring clique of over-industrious individuals.

Early in my medical school career we were brought up sharply by the tragedy of Derek R. He was a good looking, extroverted and sociable medical student with a wide circle of friends. He was passionately in love with the most beautiful girl who was well on her way to becoming a successful model. He was eighteen and she similar, and it was hard to see (in those days before the contraceptive pill) how such a relationship could stabilise rather than end in tragedy. One morning I entered the anatomy dissecting room to find my colleagues unusually silent. I was told that Derek had killed his girlfriend, presumably after an argument, and then shot himself. We analysed constantly the events that had led to this ghastly end; and we had to accept that in real life as well as on the stage, emotion may overwhelm anyone, even those who are mentally balanced and 'normal'.

The dissecting room where we learnt Anatomy was a fearsome initial experience and in retrospect a remarkable survival from the eighteenth century. The long room contained eight corpses preserved in formalin and lying on high benches. Four students were allocated to a 'body'. Each term we would dissect a different part – upper limb in the first term followed by head and neck, abdomen, thorax, lower limb and central nervous system.

The room reeked of formalin, which stained the bodies brown. The dissection to display arteries, veins, nerves and the structure and relationships of organs and tissues was carried out with a collection of surgical instruments and inevitably our protective white coats, books, paperwork and instrument roll became contaminated with the detritus of the dissecting room. We were told the bodies came from mental hospitals where inmates had died without known relatives. After the dissection, which took two years, the body remains were interred. Inevitably in the ghoulish atmosphere of the dissecting room there was much 'gallows humour' and little sense of respect for the individual represented by the body which we were dissecting. This part of the course blunted some sensibilities in us and focused our minds on the objective examination. There was no place for squeamishness or emotion. This was an important part of the medical education – to adjust so that later in the clinical setting of live patients, our reactions in the operating theatre or casualty department remained objective and unemotional. There was no room for the 'ugh' factor.

The teaching staff of St Thomas's Hospital might have stepped out of the pages of Richard Gordon's *Doctor in the House*. Of course, they were extremely able and conscientious men (I do not recall a woman on the staff) with total commitment to their work as well as their teaching. No doctor left the hospital at the end of the day if a patient in his charge needed continuing attention. Hand–over to the resident junior doctor was only when the surgery was complete; all decisions made and communicated personally to the nursing staff, and the patient's condition stable. It would have been unthinkable to hand over care because the time was 6.00 p.m.; or because the doctor had been on duty the previous night. This attitude was an important influence on the thinking of the medical students.

The consultant staff also had their extraordinary eccentricities, and often expounded extreme views to the medical students on their ward rounds. Aphorisms have stuck in my memory not so much because they are true but rather because they are epigrammatic or paradoxical. I remember a senior physician remarking, 'I have always believed that cancer is a disease of adolescence with a good prognosis for survival'; and the orthopaedic surgeon who described his speciality requiring 'the skills of a reasonably competent carpenter with two weeks' training, assisted by a chimpanzee with shaven arms'.

Most of the consultants had successful private practices in Harley Street which did not appear to conflict with their hospital work. They were consulted by the highest in the land and I remember a most distinguished physician explaining on his teaching round how you should conduct an examination on a female member of the Royal family. An elderly such person had consulted him on the previous day. 'Always carry out a rectal examination on the first consultation. It establishes the doctor-patient relationship and with Royalty the opportunity to do it on a subsequent occasion will never present itself.' The notion of Royalty consulting me once, let alone twice, seemed ridiculous, but strangely enough this advice turned out to be important – even if it did not involve Royalty. When I was qualified and in the humble role of house physician to this same consultant, we admitted an elderly but most distinguished retired surgeon – Sir Henry Letheby Tidy. He had been admitted for the investigation of a chest complaint. It was with the greatest trepidation that I introduced myself and took a history. He was friendly and patient, knowing how nervous I was. I then examined him carefully and thoroughly and wrote up my notes. When I reported my findings to the consultant his first question was: 'Did you do a rectal examination?'

'No sir, I thought it was not relevant.'

'No examination is complete if the pelvis has not been examined and the urine tested,' – and he then proceeded to complete the examination in my presence. The message that this episode taught me was never to be overawed by your patient.

One day we were on a ward round with an eminent chest surgeon. His ward was on the first floor and 'Pasty B' (as he was known) usually led the group of students up the stairs two steps at a time. On this occasion, waiting at the lift were two men with pails and mops clearly on their way to clean the floor above. Pasty B asked them why they could not climb the stairs, rather than waiting for the lift. Before they could give an explanation he ordered the students to take the mops and pails and then, in two groups, to carry the men bodily up the stairs with Pasty B leading the procession. 'Sheer laziness,' was his only comment.

At the age we were then, these men had a profound influence on our outlook. We needed role models – or heroes as they were called at that time – and the respect in which our teachers were held meant that their views on medical practice – The Art of Medicine – was listened to, accepted and eventually formed one's own approach. We were taught by example how to take a history and how to examine a patient.

The history taking was a process of listening – rather than interrogating – and with the aim of reaching a working diagnosis and 'differential diagnoses' (possible alternatives) before examination was begun. I learnt that proper care was impossible without diagnosis and that diagnosis was difficult. Wrong diagnosis might be disastrous for the patient. Sympathy and understanding of the patient's predicament was always a primary consideration but it was not enough – the doctor had taken responsibility for the patient from the start of consultation.

Armed with a differential diagnosis, the examination had to be meticulous and complete (including a rectal examination and the testing of the urine). The examination had to investigate especially those aspects related to the conditions listed in the differential diagnosis. I learnt the extraordinary variety of diseases to which mankind is susceptible. It was astonishing to discover the huge multiplicity of disorders which had to be distinguished if treatment was to be appropriate.

Laboratory or x-ray investigation was relatively limited. Investigations were expensive and consumed the time of busy pathologists and technicians. We learnt that these people should be consulted for advice rather than requested to do a test; but the outcome of investigations was always secondary to and less reliable than our own observations, taking the history and examining the patient.

Our Professor of Medicine was orthodox in one respect only. He insisted that medicine should be taught by example and apprenticeship. Thus very few lectures were given and hard facts – of which there are a great many in medicine – had to be learnt from the textbooks. These textbooks were our Bibles. They were heavy, turgid and expensive, to be learnt without any room for doubt, argument or discussion.

To acquire all the knowledge and skills in the five and a half years allotted to our medical education probably did mean that to our contemporaries we were narrow-minded and boring, but the burden of work did not prevent the development of that characteristic of Medical School humour – the practical joke.

It was considered a huge joke to find a younger student who could not answer whether it was possible to drink a pint of beer standing on your head. To prove it the unfortunate individual was set up with his legs in the air but then instead of giving him the glass to drink upside down, it was unceremoniously poured down each trouser leg.

After a Christmas party, an unpopular individual who had drunk too much was held down and encased in plaster-of-Paris leaving only holes for his eyes and mouth. Also leaving a platform upon which his genitals were arranged for display. He was propped against the wall for several hours but carried away and released before the daytime traffic in the main corridor had really begun.

I was working for a consultant who was considered by many to be pompous and aloof. He had appeared in the Honours list and received a Baronetcy. But the students and junior medical staff, far from perceiving this as bringing prestige to the hospital, considered the award only likely to make the consultant even more pompous. A junior colleague hit on a plan which seemed at the time to be hilarious. The young man rang Fortnum and Mason's and explained that we were arranging a party to celebrate the ennoblement and asked if four cases of champagne and a hundred glasses could be delivered to Central Hall before 2 p.m. the following Thursday. It was known that every Thursday this consultant lunched in the Board Room (which led off Central Hall) and emerged precisely at 2 p.m. to start his ward round. The bill was to be sent to the consultant's Harley Street address.

The word was then put round. Free champagne was available in Central Hall shortly before 2 p.m. and as expected a huge crowd of medical students had assembled drinking champagne and awaiting the arrival of Sir John. When the consultant emerged, a great shout of ironic applause went up and then everything started to go wrong and it all seemed very embarrassing and less of a joke. The consultant climbed up on to a chair and to a hushed audience said, 'I don't know who I have to thank for this generous acknowledgement . . . etc., etc.' The speech was greeted with howls of laughter but the conspirators spent the next few hours suffering the effects of too much champagne in the middle of the day and deciding how best to extricate ourselves from what by then was clearly a practical joke in poor taste. We firstly phoned the secretary in Harley Street, explained our embarrassment and told her to identify the bill and re-direct it to the ringleader; he then had a major whip-round to raise funds sufficient to pay for it. However, things did not turn out to be that easy. The bill was not identifiable from the outside and the consultant opened it. He read the contents, realised the practical joke against him, threw the bill down on his secretary's desk and said, 'Arrange for my account to pay that,' thus piling further embarrassment upon us. Fortunately, the secretary was able later to say that she had made some enquiries and the bill had been sent to Harley Street by mistake. Honour was satisfied all round but the expense incurred discouraged us from indulging in similar escapades, at least for a while.

For two years I continued to lodge with Miss Sheffield. During this time, the basics of medical science were mastered as best one could and tested in the Second MB examination. This was a major hurdle which unfortunately my closest friend, John Hughes, failed to pass. In spite of this he and I agreed to take a holiday abroad before resuming our studies in the autumn.

The plan was for three of us to go camping in France and tour the Loire valley. John Evans made up the group. I had been given an old Ford Prefect which could just accommodate us when fitted with a

Camping in France. Self, John Hughes and John Evans 1954

roof rack. John H.'s father had an old Army tent supported by wooden poles. This would provide sleeping space for two and I borrowed a small single tent. We trundled slowly across northern France each day in the evening making the repeated enquiry: '*Est-ce qu'il y a du camping près d'ici?*'

This composed about the limit of our French. Usually a friendly farmer would allow us to camp in a field nearby. On our last night we set up camp in a damp field in which an old horse was grazing. He seemed to take no notice of our intrusion. Our evening meal celebrated the success of the holiday, with much cheap wine, and we all slept soundly.

It was raining when I was woken in the early morning by much shouting from my friends' tent. The horse had been investigating this strange object. He had got into the tent, and eaten the supporting pole, bringing down sodden canvas on the sleeping occupants. We did not bother with breakfast; the tent was useless, so we packed up our other belongings and headed for home.

We had decided on holiday to give up our digs and to rent a flat together. A fourth colleague, Peter Fenton, was invited to join us. I accordingly gave notice to Miss Sheffield and in September 1956 the five of us moved into a basement flat at 6 Oakfield Street, SW6. Mr and Mrs Podger were the landlords. They must have been extremely tolerant although at the time this was not apparent to any of us. We gave parties, entertained friends and there was much coming and going. My social life blossomed as never before so that invitations flowed into Oakfield Street and the circle of acquaintances – particularly female – increased rapidly.

Peter Fenton, one of the five, had an enormous circle of friends. He was a great asset because he was perceived by mothers of eligible daughters to be 'entirely safe'. He had good manners and a comprehensive wardrobe (including white tie and tails). Above all he had social graces and the self-confidence of someone five years older.

Before we went in to the flat, Peter Fenton had organised a holiday for four of us to drive to Austria where his uncle was British Ambassador. Shortly before we set out, I met with James Kirkman who had recently returned from a holiday in Spain. When he had been asked by Customs what alcohol he was bringing back to the UK, James had declared 'one bottle of brandy'. Unfortunately for James the officer asked to see the bottle which turned out to be a *Jereboam*, not the normal bottle allowed by the Customs. James was offered two alternatives – pay the duty plus fine of £75; or have the 'bottle' confiscated. James opted for the second alternative and was then given a receipt which could be redeemed within three months so long as the brandy was taken back into Europe. When I was told this story I offered James £2 for the Customs receipt. And on arrival at Dover I asked the Customs officer to take the 'bottle' of brandy out of bond for my friends' and for my consumption during our holiday in Europe. He set off for a warehouse about two hundred yards away and we were delighted to see the officer returning walking rather slowly under the sizable burden of the substantial 'bottle' of brandy.

We were very welcome guests wherever we stayed with friends on our way to Austria. We managed to finally finish the brandy on the dockside at Calais on our return.

These were the final years of the 'Debutante Season' and presentation at Court. For at least one year I found myself a 'deb's delight' accompanying over-indulged young ladies to very grand parties, then taking them on to a nightclub (the Caballero Club or the New Coconut Grove) for a 'snog'. It seemed pretty daring at the time but was really very innocent. I was also acquiring social graces and learning to appreciate the delights of female company.

It must have been soon after my twentieth birthday in October 1955. I had been invited to a 'bottle party' where the guests supplied the drink and the host supplied the venue and the guests. Also loud music and sometimes a few eats were included. The occasion was undistinguished and I had spoken to everyone I knew at the party. I was contemplating going home either to do a bit of work or to go to bed early. Then I saw this girl sitting in a comfy armchair not talking to anyone. She seemed happy to be there even though no one was giving her any attention. And why not? She was the most beautiful person I had ever seen.

She was small and blonde. Her hair was in an 'Alice band' and curled into her neck. She was smiling as she listened to someone nearby telling a story. Clearly there was an opportunity to approach her even though we had not been introduced. I was nervous of being put down. Somehow this girl, in spite of remarkable attractiveness, seemed vulnerable and unlikely to put me down. I adopted a style of playful self-confidence and asked her permission to sit on the arm of her chair. Whether it was a conversational ploy that I had used before I really do not know but somehow I found myself discussing absurd inventions that would be convenient. The rest of the party seemed to disappear as the momentum of our conversation took off – each encouraging the other to more absurd flights of nonsense. This lovely person enjoyed absurdity, and inventive fantasy. She had the happiest laugh which I felt I had to provoke. When she laughed the lovely oval face shone. I was immediately entranced and with the encouragement I received I was spellbound by her. I learnt that her name was Sally Toller and I got her telephone number. From that time I could not get her out of my head.

I rang her the next day and made a date, which was accepted. Rapidly we got to know each other and everything I learnt about her seemed to increase her attraction. We were in love and all other relationships faded to nothing. I wanted to be with her all the time and when we were apart I thought of little else. Through the winter we went to the theatre or to restaurants. The flat was usually crowded with my colleagues but sometimes I made her supper at home. After a short time I was invited to her mother and stepfather's house for supper. I arrived inquisitive to see her home in Trevor Place and was

St Thomas's Ball 1956. Sally and self

greeted by her mother. She was a most attractive woman: vivacious, amusing and intelligent. She was not as beautiful as her daughter but I found her delightful and most welcoming.

I knew from Sally that her father had been killed in 1944. He had been a pilot in Bomber Command but never survived the war to return to his wife and three children. Sally was the oldest, David and Anthony her two younger brothers. Her father, Gerald Toller, had been brought up in China where he had learnt two Chinese dialects. At school back in England he learnt to speak French and Italian. At the outbreak of war he was a graduate student at the Sorbonne having got married shortly after coming down from Oxford. He was immediately recruited into the Intelligence Service in France. His death was a huge loss from so many points of view. He was so clearly an outstanding linguist and had every prospect of a successful career. His marriage in 1936 must have set the seal to what must have seemed an ideal future. Sally was born in 1937 in Lytham St Anne's where her father was teaching. In 1939 during the 'phoney war' her mother, Meryl, was expecting their second child and living in Paris, but decided it was safer if mother and baby daughter returned to England where David was born in November 1939. They had been lent a house in Wales by a friend of the family, Lady Rhonnda. The story was that the doctor who delivered David attended the birth on horseback and charged for his services by the number of valleys he had had to cross.

Sally spent the war years in Reigate and during the Battle of Britain her father took her onto the roof of the house to watch as if it were some sort of air display. She remembered the troops returning from Dunkirk at Reigate station and she remembered seeing her father off at the same station to go to his Royal Air Force command. Sally had a wonderful relationship with her father. When he was at home they went everywhere together. He read stories and played with her. After his death it seemed that all the happiness of childhood had depended on him. Her relationship with her mother was different. As Sally saw her mother as the feminine ideal that she had to model herself on, there were repeated hurts. Her mother was living in extremely straitened circumstances financially and sacrifices were made for the benefit of the boys but seldom for Sally. Both brothers were educated expensively at Gordonstoun but Sally was sent to a remote school in North Wales because she won a scholarship.

Meryl Toller suffered as so many wives did from the absence of her husband at war. His death was devastating, and Sally recalled her own distress at overhearing an aunt reproving her mother after his death for having married Gerald Toller who left no money to support his family. Meryl Toller met her second husband, Nigel Miskin, when she had moved to Eastbourne because the family could no longer afford to live in Reigate. Nigel Miskin was living with his grandmother in the downstairs flat, studying for his Bar exams. Nigel was nine years younger than Meryl Toller, and Sally was thirteen years younger than he. He was a handsome, self-confident and sociable man. Initially Sally welcomed her mother's newfound happiness and enjoyed being bridesmaid at the wedding at St Paul's, Knightsbridge. Two years later they moved to Trevor Place with the new baby, Charles. They could not afford help and with the increasing number of children. Sally and Meryl were very fully occupied and Nigel relied on Sally and her mother to be entirely responsible for their upbringing.

It was into this household that I stepped in the spring of 1956 for supper at Number 8, Trevor Place. I was naturally anxious to make a good impression but my efforts to present myself well were consistently flattened by Nigel. He indicated that he had looked my name up in Burke's *Landed Gentry* and in Debrett's and cast me in the role of the landed 'little Lord Austen of Godwin'. Although I did not enjoy the evening it did not dampen my enthusiasm for Sally.

As the weather allowed, Sally and I took to meeting for a picnic lunch in St James' Park. At this time Sally was working in Victoria Street for a friend of Nigel's – a bachelor aged about thirty-two. Richard Hill had been a contemporary at Charterhouse with Nigel who had asked him to give Sally a job when she completed training at secretarial school. Our lunches in St James' Park were magical. We always sat under the same tree opposite the footbridge watching the ducks and the people hurrying to and fro. I have never since been able to pass that tree without thinking of Sally and me, sitting in the sunshine, munching our sandwiches.

Sally's cousins, the Peakes, had been educated at Eton and her favourite, 'JohSeb', was teaching at Eton at that time. The family tradition was to make a day of visiting Eton on 4 June and this year I was invited to join the party, which included a close friend of Sally's – Joanna Vanderfelt. I knew that 4 June was 'OE Day', a smart occasion, part of the 'Season' with the ladies wearing hats and cotton dresses and the gentlemen in blazers and boaters – which I did not have. I contemplated buying a boater for the occasion but even the Royal Hatter in St James' Street could not find one to fit securely on my large head.

The 4 June dawned grey and cold. I presented myself at Trevor Place hatless but carrying an umbrella. Sally looked gorgeous in a white dress, 'New Look' style with pink flowers. She had a pink hat, pink gloves and a white bag. It started to rain as we drove to Eton and by the time we parked it was raining steadily. The picnic hampers were unloaded and with a spirit of forced jollity the party staggered off carrying chairs, rugs and picnic across an increasingly muddy field to a place near the Guards Band which was playing military marches. I have a vague recollection of the parade of boats with the Eton Boating Song playing repeatedly but the clearest memory is the ghastly return to the car with the ladies' hats and shoes looking frightful – soaked and muddy.

We seem not to have learnt from this outing. A few weeks afterwards it was 'OC Day' (Old Carthusian Day) at Charterhouse and a visit was planned for the OCs and Sally. Nigel, Richard Hill, Sally and I set off this time on a bright and warm day in high hopes of having an enjoyable time. What Nigel and I had not realised was that Richard Hill had taken a considerable fancy to Sally. He had accepted the invitation imagining that he would have the opportunity to advance his suit with her. In the car it was immediately obvious that my presence was resented by Richard Hill and was hence an embarrassment to Nigel Miskin. Sally fortunately had no compunction but to give me her attention. Richard Hill became increasingly sulky and finally sat in silence slightly away from our little group. The day was not a success and some weeks later Sally decided it would be best to move to another job, and thereby avoid further attention from Richard Hill.

My flatmate John Hughes had decided to organise a summer holiday in Spain. Eight of us set off by train for Sitges in Catalonia. I remember John Hughes indicating displeasure at a modest show of affection between Sally and myself on the long journey. Such were the mores in 1956 – after all we weren't even engaged! But worse was to follow. This was Franco's Spain. Bikinis were banned and the *Garda Civil* were everywhere. Sally and I one evening were sitting on a hillside watching the sunset. We were probably holding hands, which would have been disapproved of in public at that time. Suddenly an armed policeman appeared and we were accompanied at gunpoint back into town. These experiences did nothing to spoil our enjoyment of a wonderful ten days together with friends. It was probably the high point of our relationship.

I took Sally to my home in Pirbright for the weekend. My parents greeted Sally warmly but my mother created an opportunity to 'have a few words' with Sally – alone. She made it clear that my medical studies took priority over everything and that there was to be 'no question of marriage', which at that time was the only option. Living together outside marriage was not recognised as a possibility until at least ten years later.

At Sally's home things were deteriorating. She was unhappy living with her stepfather and mother and being required to look after her half brother and sister. I was more than two years from qualification

Peter Fenton, Penny, Sally and John Hughes, Sitges, Spain 1957

as a doctor and it was difficult to see how we could maintain our relationship for that length of time. I did not dare to discuss the matter with Sally. We continued to see each other every week and I was supremely comfortable and happy in her company. However, the future could not be planned so the relationship, while as strong as ever, seemed to be drifting.

Quite suddenly, early in 1957 after less than eighteen months together, Sally wrote to say that she could not see me again. She had decided to accept a plan to share a flat with a girlfriend in New York and make a new life, at least for the time being, in the USA. I was devastated. My first reaction was to try and talk her out of the decision although I knew that Sally was someone who only made a decision after she had thought of all aspects and weighed up the situation most carefully. So I decided to send her a note simply saying that I hoped that one day she would come back to me.

I told John Hughes my sad news. At this time James Kirkman, my friend from Charterhouse, was also staying in the flat. They both were very fond of Sally and gave huge support to me at that time. After talking it through with me they insisted that we went out to the pub where we continued our post–mortem and our drinking until I needed assistance to walk back to the flat.

From this experience I learnt that self-pity is an unacceptable egotism and that the relationship had been invaluable by leaving treasured memories. The sense of loss remained but the sadness was gradually submerged by new and joyful experiences and friendships, and by the increasing sense of achievement in my career.

CHAPTER 5

The resident junior doctor

IQUALIFIED AS A DOCTOR IN June 1959. This event formalised the legal recognition that I was fit to practise as a doctor taking responsibility for the health care of my patients.

During the first year after qualification ('the pre-registration year') the responsibility is mitigated to the extent that one's work is closely supervised. But steadily the awful, daunting truth dawns – as a doctor you are responsible to your patient to get it right: the right diagnosis, the right investigation and the right treatment; also the right advice and explanation, the right follow-up or referral arrangements and the right discussion with relatives; and finally a sensible and sympathetic discussion of prognosis.

At every consultation with an outpatient it is estimated that at least seven decisions have to be made, each of which has significant health implications for the patient. The stress of moving from being a medical student to being a doctor is enormous. It took me more than the pre-registration year to acquire the confidence to back my own judgement and even then there remains the need to remember that learning continues until you retire from medical practice; and over-confidence carries potentially fatal dangers – wrong diagnosis and so on.

The Finals examination was the critical hurdle – there was no form of 'continuous assessment' at that time. I had been lucky to pass my 'Obs. & Gynae' exam because I had spent the three months allocated to learn this subject reading English and Russian literature.

It is interesting to reflect that in modern times no medical student is allowed to revise only sufficient to pass the final examination at the last minute. 'Continuous assessment' imposes a uniformity on the student and discourages individual enthusiasm either for a particular specialty or for broader educational interests.

I had also been fortunate to be exceptionally well taught in General Internal Medicine as a medical student. As a result I achieved high marks in the qualifying exams in this subject and was offered the most desirable House Physician post at St Thomas's.

A sense of professionalism is not something easily taught to medical students. The medical course rightly focuses on the student acquiring information and skills. There may be lectures on ethics and humanity but the exposition of abstract concepts – like professionalism – does not inspire or even seem particularly relevant to the student and young doctor. However, the range of necessary skills for a doctor is very much wider than mere technical competence. Let us consider what we need in a doctor so that the profession can maintain standards and improve the service to patients.

It should not need to be said that a doctor should be seen to have integrity and expert knowledge within his field. Failure in these qualities is unacceptable and must lead to the likelihood of removal from clinical practice. The importance of continuing medical education has been increasingly recognised in recent times. As a result fitness to practise is dependent upon reappraisal and assessment so that competence does not decline.

However, continuing fitness to practise also depends on motivation and commitment. As a student I was aware of contemporaries who, in spite of outstanding ability and excellent examination results, lacked enthusiasm for medicine. Many gave up during the medical course and have made successful careers in other spheres. It is better to abandon a medical career early than to struggle on in a subject which does not inspire enthusiasm. There are few openings, however, for a qualified doctor other than medical practice, though Conan Doyle, A. J. Cronin and Somerset Maugham all achieved success as writers after abandoning medicine early. The cost of investing heavily in educating a doctor who then fails to provide the service to the NHS is a significant problem. I understood a wastage rate from medical school of over 5 per cent applied in my time, but it seemed mainly to indicate a failure in the selection process. Too often 'A' level students with good grades but no motivation towards medicine were encouraged to take a place at medical school because (especially to their parents) it was seen as a respectable, secure and relatively well-remunerated career. It meant that students with lower 'A' level grades but greater motivation and commitment were turned down.

Enthusiasm for the subject and motivation towards keeping up-to-date and doing your best for your patient are essential ingredients of a good doctor. The problem for a university system teaching medical students, and an NHS employing medical staff is how to maintain that motivation.

When I was a student we were influenced and inspired by the staff who taught us. Fear of failure had an effect, and competition with one's peers added to it, but the important drive developed gradually as I saw and emulated my teachers. Similarly, as a doctor the drive is to acquire the new knowledge, never fail your patient and show your colleagues your competence and commitment.

Before the changes to the management of the National Health Service initiated by Barbara Castle, the major control of hospital services took place at 'regional' level. All the hospitals within the region were given the facilities they needed by the Regional Authority who administered a substantial development budget. The Regional Medical Officer was usually a doctor with professional experience. This allowed him to assess the clinical need for a development that had been requested and to consider the relative merits of competing requests. He was advised by committees which were made up of senior doctors from hospitals throughout the region. This hierarchy of medical management and administration motivated the consultant staff. Thus a consultant would be able to develop a policy for his speciality and with the support of his colleagues he could aim to persuade the Regional Authority to provide equipment or personnel to fulfil the policy. The Regional Authority had the responsibility to encourage appropriate developments if the case had been made against competing requests. However, the importance of this structure was that it motivated hospital staff to develop the service within their specialty. As long as they delivered an improved service, so they would have the funding, and there was no bureaucracy of hospital administration, still less political targets to get in the way.

Motivation through personal responsibility for policy and developments can seldom be replaced satisfactorily by a non-medical management structure imposing sanctions on professional staff. However, the trend almost from the time I qualified has been in that direction and has led to needless waste and declining professional morale.

As a junior doctor in the 1960s I worked at the Royal Devon and Exeter Hospital. The Hospital Secretary (now renamed Chief Executive) had started his career as a hospital porter. He was probably the best senior non-medical administrator that I have ever worked with. He was a first rate judge of men, especially doctors; he was decisive and a superb administrator.

In those days the consultant's views were respected by the management. Even junior staff like myself could affect hospital policy. But it also worked the other way. I remember being astonished when the Hospital Secretary wrote to my consultant to ask him why he had been fifteen minutes late for his outpatients. However, it was right that the Secretary knew this, and correct to establish that the service must be provided properly. Relationships of mutual respect meant no offence or rancour. They also meant that the hospital was properly managed with the administration involved at every level.

After competence, motivation has always been the second most important quality in a doctor. Third, I would suggest, is judgement.

It is not enough to know the scientific facts. As a young doctor this was a particularly hard lesson to learn because one had spent up to ten years acquiring the knowledge of these scientific facts. Three years after qualification it is essential for advancement in hospital medicine to acquire by examination the 'Membership of the Royal College of Physicians'. This examination was wholly aimed at assessing your scientific knowledge. No mention was made of the exercise of judgement in the individual case. So, as a registrar, I was equipped to keep alive patients whose prognosis was hopeless and where my cutting edge treatment would inflict discomfort and impairment of dignity. Perhaps the worst result of this limited approach was the difficulty in explaining to relatives when and why treatment should be withheld or withdrawn.

When I was a newly appointed consultant I had the care of a man who showed the features of motor neurone disease with difficulties in swallowing and speaking. This terrible disease is invariably fatal and this man was expected to live a few months only. His difficulties with swallowing could be helped by a small operation to weaken a spastic muscle in his throat. The ear, nose and throat surgeon was asked to do the operation and the benefits were discussed with the patient and his family.

I was not told when he was admitted for what was very minor surgery, so I made no arrangements to visit my patient. However, three days after the operation I was informed that he had not breathed spontaneously after the operation and without asking me to explain the situation to the family they had put him on a ventilator and admitted him to intensive care. Would I now take back his medical care?

In a fatal condition such as motor neurone disease the medical management is to prepare the patient for a comfortable and dignified death. Intensive care on a ventilator increases the discomfort, reduces the dignity but most of all prolongs the physiological agony of dying. Once the step of intensive care had been taken the aim was perceived by the family and nursing staff to keep him alive. But the predicament of being conscious, unable to communicate, paralysed and dependent on complex life support with no possibility of anything other than a fatal outcome, was awful. His condition continued to deteriorate so that the little limb movement he had was gradually lost.

Rightly or wrongly, it was my judgement that life support treatment would have to be replaced with treatment to relieve symptoms, even if this meant that death was accelerated. My decision was supported by my colleagues and I embarked on the very difficult task of explaining the reasoning to the nursing staff, and to the family. The 'everything possible must be done' approach had to be brought round to accepting that the proper care of the process of dying is not necessarily prolonging life at all costs.

The need for the doctor to judge what is appropriate usually involves substantial input from the patient and his family. In cases of very severe brain damage or malignant disease, for example, teaching in recent times has tended towards scientific explanation of the likely prognosis and then leaving the patient to decide. This approach is often entirely appropriate but occasionally, especially in cases of children or young adults, it seems in my judgement to be kinder to recommend a decision which 'I would favour if it were my child'.

Humanity is the quality most of us believe we can recognise but this too varies with context – especially religious – and inevitably varies with the identification of the doctor with his patient's predicament. Islam, Buddhism and probably other religions have a sense of fatalism and acceptance certainly not shared by a Christian or agnostic society with an attitude of increasing litigation. Other serious questions arise. Is it possible for a man to understand the predicament of a woman contemplating, for example, the termination of pregnancy? Or the behavioural choices for a homosexual who is HIV positive; or the life decisions to be made by someone with cancer, especially when the doctor is in his thirties and has not (yet) seriously considered his own mortality?

It is surely accepted by any individual who has come up against serious disease that an attitude of humanity and understanding by the doctor is desirable and probably essential. However, in the list of attributes necessary in a good doctor that we demand from professional judges at interviews, from examiners in medical exams or in managers of a hospital service, it is humanity that attracts least attention.

I would suggest that humanity and a sympathetic understanding of the patient may be acquired only with time as a doctor matures within his profession. It is not acquired by learning, and teaching must mainly be by example. But humanity towards the patient and his situation must be founded on sympathy combined with respect. Without humanity the patient who is seriously ill is at best deprived of a whole dimension of their care; at worst they suffer from limited, inadequate and unsympathetic care. The old paternalistic attitude so common when I was a student has no part in the identification by the doctor with his patient's health circumstances. The doctor must be humble and have the will to be at all times in the service of his patient's medical needs.

But what of the patient's perception? Of course, only serious health problems give rise to issues such as I have been considering. It would be impertinence for a doctor to encroach on his patient's personal space and affairs where the situation did not require it. But a clinical approach which gives the explanation and prognosis, and invites questions at the same time as sharing continuing care and responsibility, leads to the perception by the patient of their doctor's humanity and sympathetic understanding.

The National Health Service in which I was employed from June 1959 was then a co-operative venture between the medical profession and the administrators appointed by the Department of Health. The professionals welcomed the salaried structure of the hospital service and were committed to giving all the time necessary to fulfil their obligations to their health service patients. The administration listened to advice from hospital staff – both medical and non-medical. A hospital consultant was judged, by his colleagues in general practice, by the quality of medical care the consultant gave to NHS patient referrals from the GP. If the GP considered the consultant care to be good he had the sanction of referring the occasional private patient. This structure created a cohesion between the separate elements of the service that was enormously to the benefit of the patient services. In particular the quality of consultant care in hospital was judged by the GP, not by the length of the waiting time for outpatients or surgery, but by the spoken communications of the patient with their General Practitioner, and the outcome of the treatment recommended.

Everyone in the NHS at that time was conscious and proud of the fact that the NHS provided the best standard of medical care available anywhere in the world. I shall return to the reasons why, in my view, the quality of care has so declined, in spite of huge advances in medical treatment, and massive investment (see Appendix).

My first six months after qualification were spent in the Casualty Department of St Thomas's Hospital. Like all such departments we operated an 'open door' policy where any patient who wanted treatment could present themselves and be seen by a doctor. The department only coped through the personality and experience of 'Sister Cas'.

When the team of fourteen Casualty Officers took over from the night staff at 8.00 a.m., Sister Cas was at a table by the door sorting patients into categories. The great majority were simple injuries or infections. Any patient suspected of a fracture of a long limb bone, or with chest pain, abdominal pain, sudden headache or loss or disturbance of consciousness was given priority to be seen by a Casualty Officer, prior to being seen by the RAP or RAS. These were doctors with at least five years' experience from whom I learnt so much about the efficient immediate care of emergency cases. Sister Cas was feared by doctors, nurses and patients alike. As with a good schoolteacher she was aware of everything going on in the department. Any untidiness, slacking or frivolity was pounced upon by her shouting at the top of her voice, 'Dr Jones, clear up that mess immediately.' We learnt how to sew up skin lacerations, apply plaster casts and lance abscesses. We used simple anaesthesia (gas, oxygen and chloroform) through a face mask, and in heavily built patients this seemed only to render them confused and aggressive rather than unconscious. There are memories of my chasing a semi-anaesthetised burly Smithfield porter who had an abscess on his buttock that needed lancing. The poor man was stark naked on a couch with a colleague holding a mask over his face while I prepared to open the boil. Suddenly he pushed us both aside and charged through the curtains roaring his displeasure to the astonished benches of waiting patients.

Night duty came round once a week and was always very busy. It meant twenty-four hours on duty and then six hours off (8.00 a.m. to 2.00 p.m.) before doing a short afternoon (2.00 p.m. to 6.00 p.m.). Generally it was about 1.00 a.m. before one could go to the small bedroom provided, and during the night we would be called two or three times to see a patient who had presented at Casualty. Although there was inevitably considerable sleep deprivation, I firmly believe this did not lead to errors. It must certainly have made us more peremptory and impatient especially with cases whose needs did not seem urgent. But the worst effect was unexpected. When on duty at night I would get to sleep expecting to be called; and then dreamed that I *had* been called but had failed to get up . . . and then gone back to sleep. This dream was so vivid that I would wake, get up and dress hurriedly only to find on arrival in the Casualty Department that the night nursing staff had not called me after all.

Although violence towards hospital staff by patients has increased enormously, it was something we had to be aware of. I remember a colleague being attacked with a cut-throat razor by a drunken patient, only saving himself by throwing a 'Lan Air Cell' blanket over the individual. Drunkenness was the cause of much of the injury and violence seen in the department and reflected the social conditions in Lambeth at that time.

At the end of my time as a Casualty Officer I took two weeks holiday to go ski-ing in Austria. I had not seen Miss Elliott for many years, but I had kept in touch, and realised that she was looking after the children of a German landowner in Bavaria. I therefore wrote to ask whether it would be possible visit her at the weekend while I was so close.

I took the train to Munich and was met by Miss Elliott. And I began to realise that the establishment was rather grand when we were driven by the chauffeur to the *Schloss Seefeld*. The house was a pinnacled Bavarian castle and I was shown to my bedroom suite by the butler. I had come only with a small bag of pyjamas and washing things. My rooms were extremely cold. In the morning I wanted a bath but had to walk through my sitting room to get to the enormous bathroom. I put on my only shoes to make the journey and while I was in the bath I could hear the butler, who must have been listening at my door, come into the bedroom and search for my shoes so that they could be cleaned. After several minutes he gave up and I was left to go down to breakfast in dirty shoes. I was seated next to the grandmother, Baroness Walbott. In my efforts to make polite conversation, and knowing that she and her husband had fled from Hungary when the Nazis invaded, I asked, 'In what part of Hungary did you used to live?'

To which she replied, 'Let me explain. If you travelled by boat down the Danube from Vienna, the first eleven castles you passed belonged to my family.'

It was hard to know what to say next.

After my six months in Casualty I moved on to resident house jobs. I did three such 'jobs' at St Thomas's – successively, House Physician to Dr Goadby's firm, Paediatric House Physician and finally Neurology House Physician. Each stint lasted six months. One had thirty-six hours off duty every two weeks (Saturday midday to Sunday midnight) but was effectively otherwise on-call day and night. However, it was a pleasant routine. The hospital provided comfortable single bedrooms and we dined and had club facilities in College House in the Central Block of the old Nightingale building, a distance from the patients' ward blocks. The dining room was especially spacious, two floors up with windows overlooking the Thames. When I was first resident, uniformed stewards served our meals and we could help ourselves to a glass of beer provided free by a philanthropic local brewery. This comfortable and privileged lifestyle changed during my two years 'on the house'. Evidently the cost of providing these facilities to junior resident doctors was considered excessive by the hospital administration and plans were drawn up, without consultation, to install an aluminium cafeteria counter where we would queue up for our food. Needless to say the proposed break with a fine tradition in a historic teaching hospital was considered retrograde, but we seemed powerless to affect the planners. However, a plot was hatched.

The medical staff decided to give a party to celebrate the new facilities when the work was complete. This surprised the adminis-tration because they had received complaints and criticism of the plans from many quarters. It was a most successful if rather noisy party. At midnight as Big Ben struck, the cry went up: 'Destroy,

destroy!' and the slightly intoxicated junior staff fell on the cafeteria, pulled it apart and threw the pieces out of the windows where they crashed onto the concrete basement area with a most satisfying sound. The job done, the party continued.

Of course we lost the battle but had made our point. A new cafeteria was installed in due course (without penalty to the destroyers) and the quality of life for the resident junior staff was never again so comfortable.

The nursing staff at St Thomas's were unequalled in the quality of nursing care that they provided. The hierarchy was headed by Matron who was seen as the direct reincarnation of Florence Nightingale herself. She was never without the company of her two acolytes or under-matrons. Every morning this retinue visited every ward to take a report from the Ward Sister.

The uniform of the nursing staff had not changed since Victorian times. Dark blue (pale blue stripes for ordinary nurses) elegantly cut uniform dresses with starched white collar and cuffs, and pinafore with a dark blue canvas belt and ornate silver buckle. Black stockings, low rubber heeled sensible shoes and crowning glory – a starched and goffered lace hat. Not only did this uniform make the plainest girl look tidy and professional, but it also discouraged patients and junior doctors from taking liberties.

The Ward Sisters were the real force in the organisation. They each had complete responsibility for every aspect of the running of the ward. They had to organise the nursing staff rotas and teaching; the passage of information on each individual patient; the recording of observations and of requests by patients and their families; and significantly (for these things have now been taken from them) responsibility for meals and their distribution, cleaning the ward, tidying bed tables and clearing flowers. Ward Sisters were usually unmarried and in their forties or fifties. They were personally committed to the job they did and this commitment inspired the student nurses and SRNs working on the ward. Every morning I, as House Physician, would do a ward round (after Matron had departed) with the Ward Sister. At this time she had her sleeves rolled down and starched white cuffs in place. Never once did I fail to get information on a patient's observations and condition.

When I was working as a Paediatric House Physician, the Sister to the children's ward provided huge support in decision-making on the ward round. She was someone who had many years' experience of caring for sick children and thus knew my job far better than I did. She was invariably courteous and patient, tactful in her suggested advice and content to accept my clumsy medical analysis. At the end of the round before rolling up her sleeves to get back to work she would give me a cup of coffee and a biscuit in her ward sitting room, while we engaged in mutually respectful, polite conversation. It was all very civilised, efficient and unhurried – and it worked.

We did two ward rounds each day, a detailed visit to every in-patient on our firm in the morning accompanied by the Ward Sister and twice a week by the Registrar; and a less detailed night round visit to discuss the patients' progress and night care with the night nursing staff. On a night round to the children's ward I noticed a slim, pleasant and attractive nurse who had just taken over as Nurse-in-Charge. A ward round was a time for discussing medical matters and not a time for dalliance. However, my night round lasted a little longer after this first encounter and I lingered over my hot milk and biscuit provided by this delightful girl.

I had had no serious relationship for about three years and I had committed myself absolutely to a demanding training and career. But now suddenly wider aspirations were starting to open up. Towards the end of 1960 one of the friends who had shared our flat was Peter Davis. He was a most able and hard working medical student with a droll and rather vulgar sense of humour. In due course he went on to follow a successful career as Consultant Plastic Surgeon at St Thomas's Hospital. His family had some connection with the East Essex Hunt, which had its Hunt Ball every year in Chelmsford Town Hall. I was invited to join a party that Peter was organising and invited Rosemary Green to come as my partner. Rosemary had been a long-standing friend with no romantic attachment to whom I had been introduced by John Hughes' sister Delia. The two of them had been at school together in North Wales, coincidentally that same school where Sally Toller had gone. Rosemary worked as a personal assistant to the distinguished journalist Tim Utley, who was blind. He relied considerably on Rosemary in her work because he depended on being read all the relevant newspapers and journals every day so that he could prepare his columns in the *Daily Telegraph*. Rosemary was wonderful company, and I looked forward to a pleasant if slightly conventional evening.

She and I drove to the East Essex Hunt Ball and met up with the party of ten friends. When we were gathering I was surprised to notice that Peter had brought as his partner the night nurse from the children's ward, and dressed for the Ball she looked fabulous. I wanted to talk and dance with her but in those days social conventions and etiquette were powerful. I knew that I had to look after Rosemary and Peter was understandably possessive about his beautiful partner. There was no opportunity to dance with her and it was not until the mandatory Eightsome Reel that I found myself able to put an arm around Jane's waist, and look into her eyes. She always remembered the moment. It is remarkable how sensitive to nuance we were in those days – almost reminiscent of Jane Austen.

How I got hold of Jane Himely's telephone number I cannot remember but I was most anxious not to let her memory of our brief (very brief) encounter to fade. My uncle Reade had a favourite London restaurant where he had taken me on several occasions. Scott's Oyster Bar was at the top of Haymarket. I knew the table by the window on the first floor and booked it for my first date with Jane. She was entrancing, vivacious, funny, and very beautiful. We then saw much of each other and it slowly became clear that the relationship was going to be serious.

There was a slight hiccup to our romance because I had committed myself to a skiing holiday in December and it was too late for Jane to join the party. Perhaps this was a good thing because it allowed a short spell apart to contemplate what our relationship meant. When we met again on my return we both knew that we were committed to each other.

In 1961 I was working as a Neurological Senior House Officer. This was the most prestigious junior resident post working for two consultants – both with national reputations.

J. StC. Elkington ('Jack') had been appointed to St Thomas's Hospital at the early age of twenty-eight and to the National Hospital for Neurology shortly after. He had contributed to the classic *Price's Textbook of Medicine* and was a renowned teacher. As a clinician he was an obsessive and brilliant diagnostician. He seemed never to forget a case that he had seen and could apply his extensive experience to decisions in the clinic or on the ward.

Jack Elkington was sixty-one when I started working for him. I had to 'clerk' (take a history), examine and arrange investigation for all neurological admissions. I then had to present these cases to the two ward rounds each week. I was not allowed to refer to notes at my presentation. At first the feat of memory to call to mind every detail of some fifteen patients seemed formidable but surprisingly, within two weeks the task seemed effortless. There was, however, no encouragement or approbation for one's endeavours, only the expectation that everything would be done faultlessly. I had not, until that time, worked quite so hard or learnt quite so much, at the same time as conducting a passionate romance with my lovely Jane.

Over tea, after a ward round, Dr Elkington (who was a bachelor) observed that no doctor could expect to be successful in neurology if he married before the age of thirty. I was then twenty-five and planning to propose to Jane at Easter when I was staying with her parents at Bovey Tracey. Whether Dr Elkington knew that he had created serious turmoil in my plans it is difficult to know but he helped considerably by telling me a few weeks later that if I wanted to I could, in his opinion, make a successful neurologist. For obvious reasons, I chose to accept this rather than the earlier advice. But to be told by someone I admired that I could pursue that ambition was a critical turning point in my career. I abandoned the possibility of paediatrics, which I enjoyed; and the softer option of the security of General Practice. I started to prepare myself for the major hurdle of the membership examination (MRCP) and I started to look for a job that would advance my training in the specialty.

Jane and I became engaged at Easter, and celebrated with a cream tea at the Manor House Hotel at Chagford. Dr Elkington had gone on holiday to Rhodes when I returned to work so I was able to spend more time with Jane. Only a few days later, however, we heard that Dr Elkington was seriously ill, jaundiced and in a coma, and was to be flown back immediately. He was admitted under the care of Professor Sharpey Schafer and the Registrar to the Professor was no less than Dr Elkington's nephew, Stephen Elkington. He was put in a side ward and there was a flurry of investigation, assessment and treatment. No diagnosis was immediately evident. Professor Sharpey Schafer therefore contacted the formidable 'Liver Queen', Professor Sheila Sherlock, at the Hammersmith Hospital. Shortly after, the two professors were seen sailing down the main corridor of St Thomas's pursued by some twenty acolytes discussing their prestigious patient.

'Does he drink, Sharpey?'

'Not as much as you do, Sheila!'

After the consultation the diagnosis was cirrhosis of the liver. But this diagnosis, made by the highest in the land, was overturned neatly by Stephen Elkington who, like me, had learnt well the basics of clinical examination.

Haemochromatosis is a rare chronic disorder in which iron is accumulated in the body leading to organ damage over many years. The liver and the pancreas are two organs critically damaged and this causes the development of jaundice and diabetes. Haemochromatosis is an important diagnosis because, even in 1961, it was potentially curable with treatment to remove chemically the iron from the body.

Until Stephen Elkington did so, no one had tested the patient's urine. Dr Jack Elkington was not known to be a diabetic but Stephen Elkington's full examination proved that he was, and that Professor Sherlock's diagnosis was wrong. There was potential for effective treatment. Sadly, the diagnosis was too late. Although Dr Elkington returned to work he had another bout of liver failure after I had finished working for him and died about two years later.

I owe to Jack Elkington and to Dr Reggie Kelly (the other consultant neurologist) a great debt for opening my eyes to the fascination and challenge of this specialty. Neurology is a subject so vast that you can never know it all. The practice of Clinical Neurology demands obsessive attention to detail and the exercise of skills in history taking and physical examination that are only learnt slowly and laboriously. But through the advent of a revolution in medical treatment and investigation, Clinical Neurology has become a specialty where treatment is available, in most cases, and this treatment is critical to the patient's health and prognosis.

CHAPTER 6

The magical year in Devon

WE WERE MARRIED ON THE 'glorious twelfth' of August 1961. The ceremony was at Chelsea Old Church with Canon Leighton Thompson officiating. Jane's parents were still in Malaysia, so Jane had to organise the reception herself. It was held in a beautiful house in Hamilton Place, and Jane was proud to find reduced price magnums of Champagne from an Italian 'off-licence' near Waterloo.

Our honeymoon I organised. The plan was to cross the Channel by air from Lydd airport, drive to Paris and catch the car-carrying train to Biarritz. All went well until I had to leave Jane on the platform at Gare Austerlitz where our Pullman sleeper was, and go to load the car onto its carriage in a siding. I returned to find Jane sobbing her heart out in our sleeping compartment. She was overcome with homesickness and the loneliness of a new life where she was dependent on someone she had only known for less than a year. We recovered with much comforting, and slept well, sharing the lower single bunk.

The first night of our honeymoon in the Pyrenees was a disaster. I had planned to drive to a small town where a comfortable hotel could put us up. But when we drove into the town it was *en fête* and packed with people. The hotel was full, our room had been let to someone else, and I had to insist that Monsieur ring round and find us somewhere to stay.

Half an hour later he approached us with the upturned hands and shrugged shoulders of the disappointed Frenchman. The only room available was at a farmer-friend's house. We agreed the arrangement – there was no alternative.

Our 'bedroom' was upstairs in a barn. It was large, hot, and full of stored furniture including a double bed. Our host and his wife were both in their eighties and spoke only an incomprehensible patois.

We woke after an uncomfortable night, dressed quickly, and prepared to leave. With some difficulty I discovered that we would be charged the equivalent of 2s. 4d. for the room. But the worst result

Going away – wedding 12 August 1961

we discovered only the next day. We were both covered in flea-bites. The whole honeymoon we were scratching at the 'fleas that tease in the High Pyrenees'.

We were pleased that no one asked us whether we had enjoyed our honeymoon. It was considered an inappropriate question.

Before the wedding I had had to consider carefully the possibilities for my next job. A training for a specialty such as neurology involved a succession of jobs lasting between six and eighteen months in different hospitals. Many of the best jobs were resident and involved the supervision of the junior medical staff. I had been offered just such an appointment. Against accepting it was the fact that it was compulsorily resident with only alternate weekends off. In favour was that it was at the Royal Devon and Exeter Hospital and a relatively short distance from Bovey Tracey where Jane's parents were to live. But it seemed a job likely to progress my career and we agreed to go for it. Before the wedding, like all brides, Jane had been exceptionally busy. Her first task was to persuade the senior nursing staff of St Thomas's that she should resign her job. They had plans for her promotion and were miffed to find that she considered marriage to be a higher calling than a nursing career!

She then started the search for somewhere to live in Exeter and was exceptionally lucky to find a flat to rent only a hundred yards from the hospital. This meant there was the possibility of stretching the residency rules of my job. Instead of spending the first year of our marriage in monastic separation we were able to embark on a most unexpected pregnancy.

The flat was tiny and situated on the main Topsham Road. Our bedroom was so small and the bed so big that to pull out a drawer you had to lie on the bed and get your legs out of the way. It was a Victorian house owned by a kindly quiet couple who lived downstairs. The bathroom had probably remained unchanged since the house was built a hundred years before and it delivered hot water through a remarkable gas geyser. When the hot tap was turned on there was a sudden explosion as the gas lit, followed by the roar of flame heating the water. Friends visiting us would reappear from the bathroom white-faced with fear, having thought their last moment had come as they prepared to wash their hands.

We had a dining table in one corner of the sitting room and it was here that Jane exercised her aspiration to be the perfect hostess.

One day a friend who had visited to give a lecture was invited to dinner. It was the first time we had had the opportunity to display our impressive wedding presents. Preparations for the meal had started in the early morning but when I arrived from work, less than an hour before the guests were due, Jane was in tears. A chocolate sauce essential for the chosen pudding had inexplicably curdled and was inedible.

As medical students and bachelors sharing a flat we had each had to cook meals for all on a rota. This had given me a very few basic cooking skills. One of these (of which I was very proud) was my white sauce. I could cover lamb, veal or chicken in white sauce; and likewise it could be used to disguise leftovers of faded cauliflower or leeks.

Without hesitation and ignoring the sobbing from my wife, I seized the derelict chocolate sauce and added it to my hastily-made white sauce in which sugar rather than salt had been used. The result was deemed by all to be a triumph and for several weeks I enjoyed a reputation to be proud of.

At the hospital the opportunity was available to join the local golf club. This was a very modest affair with an uninteresting flat course in the Exeter suburbs. But I discovered that subsidised club membership brought an important advantage. Apparently all the golf clubs in Devon had signed an agreement for their members to have one round of golf on each Devonshire course each year. With three friends, I joined the Club for £3 and every alternate Saturday we set off with wives and picnic to a different golf course around the county. It has given me a wonderful knowledge of Devon and many very happy memories of those times.

The Royal Devon and Exeter Hospital was then situated adjacent to the Cathedral Close in a magnificent Georgian building. Exeter was, and is, a wonderful city in which to live and practise and consequently it attracted GPs and hospital staff of a very high calibre. My boss 'Barney' Alcock was a good example. A man of intellect and great humanity, he practised neurology to the highest standards in spite of limited access to special x-ray facilities. Without these tests diagnosis had to be based on meticulous observation, record keeping and follow-up. Thus symptoms which might be caused by a spinal tumour but were more likely due to a disc would be repeatedly reassessed and as soon as any feature pointed to an evolving tumour, then and only then would the patient be referred to the neurosurgeon visiting from Bristol (once a month) for expensive, and often painful, investigation. This was an important lesson in the proper and economical use of resources and on reliance on clinical methods to make a diagnosis. The workload carried by the consultant staff was considerable – ward rounds, out-patient clinics, ward consultations in hospitals as far away as Barnstaple and Torquay, as well as regular monthly sessions at outlying hospitals. After an evening outpatient clinic, it was usual for the consultant physicians to have two or three domiciliary consultations with General Practitioners. I thought I had worked hard as a medical student. I had to work much harder as a House Physician and even more as a Registrar. I could see that there was going to be no let-up if I ever achieved consultant status.

Every week the consultant pathologist presented an autopsy case which illustrated an interesting or important medical fact. A case that has stuck in my memory concerned a man who was well-known in his public house for his thirst and for his inability to pay for his round of drinks. He suffered from a spinal condition where the vertebrae fuse into a solid column of bone, known as ankylosing spondylitis. This man had discovered, presumably in a fight, that it was difficult to knock him out. This could be explained medically because a blow to the chin needs to cause abrupt extension of the neck to cause loss of consciousness. Our patient was a big man and his technique was to challenge the company in the pub by allowing any individual to hit him on the chin as hard as they could provided that, in return, either they submitted to a similar blow or bought our friend a pint of cider.

To hit on the chin with bare knuckles a heavy man with ankylosing spondylitis is like hitting a solid wall. However, in Exeter at that time there were regular sadistic takers and few, if any, agreed to accept the counter-blow. One day an individual hit him so hard on the chin that a ligament at the top of his spine ruptured and he fell to the floor, killed instantly by the blow. The assailant had a difficult case to answer in Court. We learnt from the post mortem demonstration that this ligament is selectively weakened in cases of ankylosing spondylitis.

My income as a Registrar was not generous and soon after starting in Exeter, Jane was looking for a job. She had just found work as a dental nurse when she realised she was pregnant. Fortunately pregnancy is no bar to dental nursing and she was able to take the job and usefully supplement our income. A few months later I developed toothache which we concluded was psychological because I was jealous of her work. However, it turned out to be unerupted wisdom teeth which needed removal. Jane was landed with the unpleasant task of assisting the dentist while he removed my wisdom teeth under local anaesthetic. The day appointed for this operation was late June, and her expected delivery date was mid August. The weather was very hot. The dentist was not confident and not reassuring. I remember Jane trying to hold my head down on the headrest while the dentist tugged this way and that with both hands grasping the dental forceps. It may be my imagination but at one stage he had his knee on my chest to hold me down. No ligaments ruptured, the teeth came out and I can remember the dentist, who by that stage was sweating profusely, removed his shirt and washed to the waist at the sink. Most importantly this episode did not provoke premature labour and Jonathan was born some seven weeks later.

Jonathan 1962, Topsham Road, Exeter

The end of summer 1962 found us going for long happy walks in the Devonshire countryside and on Dartmoor with our small son carried in a blanket or pushed in a pram. Jane's parents in Bovey were an enormous help but an attempt to indicate our gratitude misfired badly.

The University Theatre in Exeter was putting on a production of *Abelard and Heloise* with Diana Rigg in the role of Heloise. My father-in-law was the product of a strict Christian upbringing. He drank little and smoked the occasional pipe but was never known to swear or to give way to any vulgar still less lustful or blasphemous talk. What Jane and I did not know was that this play involved nudity, sodomy, blasphemy, rape and castration all enacted on stage. The University Theatre had the stage at the same level as the floor in the stalls. We were in the front row of the stalls and so had nudity and all else almost in our laps.

My in-laws were horrified and froze in their seats, but in our company and seated where we were they felt unable to walk out. They had driven us to the theatre and planned to drive back to Bovey after the play. For the first and sadly the last time ever, my father-in-law poured forth a torrent of outrage. It lasted all the way from the theatre car park to their house near Manaton. Jane and I sat silently in the back but when we were on our own we could only see the funny side of the episode.

Our first Christmas as a married couple had been spent with Jane's parents and two sisters in Devon. Christmas 1962 was my parents' turn so was spent in Surrey. On Boxing Day we went beagling and after a lunch in the pub the temperature began to fall rapidly. We planned to drive to Devon and spend New Year's Eve with Jane's parents. So the next day, in freezing, bright weather we set off in the Morris Minivan on the five hour drive.

My job in Exeter had finished before Christmas and we had decided that I would not take a full-time job for three months but instead work for my examinations and take locums to earn a bit of money. We were to live rent-free in a house belonging to Jane's cousin who had been posted abroad. The house was in West Wickham in the suburbs of South London. We planned to drive from Devon to London on New Year's Day 1963.

It started to snow before New Year's Eve but by the morning of New Year's Day six inches had fallen in Devon which we were told was one of the least-affected counties.

I stubbornly refused to accept persuasion not to embark on the journey and early that morning we drove off with our possessions packed in our Minivan with Jonathan in his carrycot wedged under the roof. It was an alarming journey. Main roads were closed by snow or the police. Lorries had slid into ditches further blocking the way and all the time heavy snow continued to fall. Ten hours after setting out we reached West Wickham and had to carry everything through two feet of snow to the front door of the empty house, but we were there and the most stressful chapter of my life so far was about to unfold.

CHAPTER 7

The postgraduate years

'WELL WE MADE IT,' SAID JANE somewhat disconsolately as she trudged across the deep snow towards our second marital home. We came to West Wickham through the extreme generosity of a cousin. But – it was awful. It was the epitome of 1930s suburban development with diamond pane windows and open coal fires, steep stairs, pokey rooms. We were miles from the shops and knew no one in the area to ask advice. And the *cold*! The deep snow didn't thaw until 6 March. At night ice formed inside the bedroom window and we had to get up every three hours to flush the loo to prevent the pipes freezing. And most remarkably, when I stoked up the fire to get a good blaze, black smuts formed in the air and gently settled on everything including the baby and us. I have never been able to explain the phenomenon; perhaps it was the coal we were burning.

I was working for my Membership examination (MRCP) travelling on icy suburban trains (two changes) to the London Hospital. I knew I had only one chance of passing the exam – we couldn't afford unemployment for another three months and if I failed it would probably be best to emigrate and find work abroad – maybe South Africa.

These were the so-called carefree 1960s. The Beatles were about to emerge and people of our age were starting to experiment with drugs. The contraceptive pill had led to a great loosening of morals. Pop music was the rage and pirate radio ships broadcast it from the Thames estuary. But all these joys seemed to pass us by. We were a boring married couple trying to cope with a small baby in borrowed and unsuitable accommodation.

Gloomy thoughts of this sort were compounded when I returned one evening to be told by Jane that she had seen a surgeon that day and had been told that she had a tumour on her jaw. It needed removal so that they could find out what it was.

Jonathan was six months old. Jane was struggling in the worst winter since 1947 and I was struggling to prepare myself for a crucial exam. And now this! Clearly the surgery must be done as soon as possible. Knowing our predicament the surgeon arranged for Jane to go into a small private hospital in Haslemere and he charged no fees. Meanwhile Jonathan was left with my parents and I signed on for 'the dole' (unemployment benefit).

The day after the operation the surgeon explained that it was a 'pre-malignant' mixed parotid tumour of the jaw and he had removed a substantial block of tissue from around the tumour to minimise the risk of recurrence. Jane had a face swollen like a watermelon but the surgery had been done entirely through her mouth and there were no external scars. Things seemed to be looking up. Jonathan came back to us none the worse for the separation from his mother (my parents also survived) and over Easter I obtained a remunerative GP locum job. When in April I passed my examination it seemed that all our troubles were over.

There followed frantic house-hunting for Jane and job hunting for me. We were both successful. Jane found a third floor flat (no lift) in a mansion block in Maida Vale and I found a registrar job back at St Thomas's Hospital. I was working for the neurologists so the duties were familiar from my previous SHO job. The SHO now was David Owen (later Lord Owen). He was campaigning in Torrington on alternate weekends off at the same time as doing his clinical work. We scarcely took seriously his enthusiasm for politics until two years later when he won the Plymouth seat for Labour and thereafter abandoned a career in medicine where he had shown considerable promise.

My Uncle Reade had been ill for several years with a variant of Parkinson's disease. I had arranged for him to see Dr J. StC. Elkington but in those days treatment with drugs was relatively ineffective and brain surgery was reserved for younger people than Uncle Reade. When he died in 1962 he had seen Jonathan who was named after him. He left to me a legacy, and his house and contents. We were, therefore, able to furnish our new flat in Maida Vale.

After four months at St Thomas's I moved to a registrar job at the Middlesex Hospital working for two neurologists. One was highly regarded, the other greatly feared. I probably only got the job because there were few applicants.

Michael Kremer was, at that time, senior neurologist at the Middlesex Hospital. He had qualified in the 1930s and had served as a doctor in the war. After the war he trained as a neurologist and was appointed at an early age to a consultant position at the National Hospital for Neurology and at the Middlesex. He had married early in his training and within months of the wedding his wife suffered a spinal injury and was paralysed from the neck down. Michael Kremer was never able to accept the prestigious resident training posts at the National because throughout his career his first priority was the care of his paralysed wife. My recent troubles seemed small beside his.

I had never met anyone who worked such long hours and yet showed so much patience and understanding towards his patients. At the end of a full working week we started Michael Kremer's clinic at 2.00 p.m. on Friday and finished around 6.00 p.m. The ward round went on until about 8.00 p.m. On Saturday morning, we first dictated letters from the Friday clinic and then assembled to continue the ward round at 10.00 a.m., usually finishing between 3.30 p.m. and 4.00 p.m. The exhausted junior staff were at last able to go to their families. But Michael would have accumulated through the morning scraps of paper with details from the nursing staff or secretaries of NHS domiciliary consultations, which he would then set out to do.

This commitment to the job and to his patients was an important example to us all. Not only was Kremer a wise diagnostician and a good neurologist; his patients and staff trusted and admired him and his overall manner, far from being pompous or overbearing, was jokey and friendly. If he had a fault it was his slightly tiresome childish sense of humour.

Professor Roger Gilliatt was very different. He was the son of the Queen's obstetrician. He had been a brilliant student gaining high academic honours. He had fought in the Italian campaign and won an MC, and had finally made a reputation in collaboration with Tom Sears (of whom more later) by applying physiological techniques for nerve conduction measurements to studies in human patients. Incidentally he was best man to Anthony Armstrong Jones (Lord Snowdon) at his wedding to Princess Margaret.

We all recognised that not only had Roger been born with the proverbial silver spoon but he had also worked his way to a position of great power at a relatively early age. The Professor of Neurology at the National (it was he) was the senior Chair in the specialty and carried considerable power to make or break careers, especially those of his junior staff like me. We all knew the names of individuals who had worked for Roger but earned his displeasure. They never got another job and had to emigrate. Thirty years later some of these individuals have had extremely successful academic careers as neurologists (e.g. Donald Calne) and medical writers (e.g. Oliver Sacks) in the New World. But at that time I knew that working for Roger Gilliatt might either start or finish my career. There was no middle way.

After his ward round and over a cup of tea the conversation would go: 'How old are you, Godwin-Austen?'

'Nearly thirty, Sir.'

'Hmm . . . you must be ready to take a consultant job by thirty-five. No-one can get an appointment after thirty-five. Are you married?' etc etc.

In those days girls were told there was no hope of marriage after twenty-five and I understood then what they must have felt like. But I was fortunate to gain the backing of both consultants. They had considerable influence and exerted it on my behalf at many critical points in the next five years.

At the Middlesex, however, I had two unexpected problems. The contraceptive pill had been available on prescription since about 1963 but there were much-discussed 'dangers' and most married couples used the more traditional forms of contraception. In October 1963 Jane became accidentally pregnant for the second time. We had just seemed to be overcoming a series of serious problems . . . *and now this*.

At the same time I began to be aware of pain in my left hip. The pain slowly got worse and without saying anything to anybody I wrote myself up for an x-ray. The consultant radiologists had teaching sessions open to junior staff when they reported on the films of the day. I therefore went along and sat in the group listening to the radiologist who was going to report on my hip x-ray.

'The upper end of the femur contains an abnormality about 1cm in diameter with the appearances of a deposit from Hodgkin's Disease. Next . . .'. At that time Hodgkin's Disease was untreatable and fatal.

I made my excuses, left the room and sat in an office trying to gather my thoughts. 'Would I survive to see my second child?' . . . 'What would happen to Jane and Jonathan?' . . . 'What would happen to me?' And I remember a distant radio inanely blaring: 'She loves you, yeah, yeah, yeah . . .'

My operation removed the upper end of the thigh bone and I watched Wimbledon with my leg in traction unable to stand. I have never wanted to watch Wimbledon again. The result was not Hodgkin's Disease but a benign tumour and I was just off crutches when Alice was born.

The birth was not without incident. Jane had had antenatal care from a distinguished obstetrician who gave his services free to the wives of colleagues (his 'fur coat clinic'). This was the rule in those days. However, when she went into labour on 30 July he was away and the baby was delivered by a midwife. I had taken Jane to hospital and then taken Jonathan, again, to the care of my parents. The baby – Alice – arrived quickly and I was returning to greet the new arrival armed with champagne. I was driving fast (to overtake a bus) in the middle lane of a three-lane road when my windscreen suddenly shattered and I had no vision forwards. I could only come to a halt in the middle of the road with traffic pouring past me on both sides in opposite directions.

I was still shaking when I reached the side room Jane had been given. She lay there as white as the pillow case trying to smile but obviously very ill. Blood transfusions were running fast and nurses were hurrying in and out.

The 'fur coat' care that she had been given included leaving her unobserved in a single room while the midwife went to have a cup of tea. Jane very nearly died of a post-partum haemorrhage. But she didn't die and nor did I. We were thankful to God for deliverance from our various crises and closer to each other having come through them. Indeed it was better than that. We had come through them and had gained two healthy children. What a responsibility but what blessings!

Although I had a job, and a regular income, the perception was one of serious poverty. Junior doctors in those days were not paid well and the job contract lasted twelve months at most. The lack of security for the family man, as I then was, gave a palpable fear that we would not cope with the next crisis, and there was the constant worry of obtaining the next job. We were all aware of how competitive it was to obtain employment that led to promotion. There was a constant loss of well-trained good doctors who were forced either to apply for jobs that did not lead to promotion within the specialty; or who got jobs abroad and then found that they could not get back into British medicine. Among my contemporaries nearly 50 per cent of the people who wanted to become a career neurologist failed to do so. Out of five consecutive neurological registrars at the Middlesex Hospital only two, of whom I was one, achieved a consultant post in the United Kingdom. Their capabilities were every bit as good as mine and in several cases much better.

The only way that we could improve our chances was to make a reputation by publishing work in the medical journals. 'Publish or perish' was the motto. Roger Gilliatt indicated that I must publish three papers at least every year until I became a consultant. In a clinical job no time was set aside for research or writing, and little help was available to find research projects on the ward or in the clinic. Although I did not appreciate it at the time, the pressure to investigate and publish focused the mind on the frontiers of knowledge in medicine. I gradually realised that knowledge is finite and it is one of the responsibilities of every doctor at whatever stage of his career to discover the limits of information and to consider how the scientific method can be used to push back those limits for the benefit of all patients in the same predicament.

Thus many hours in the evening were spent reading through the literature on a subject in the library and then considering how to construct an investigation that would enable a conclusion to be reached that answered a question relevant to medical care.

My first publication was in 1967 and reported the case of a lady who had gone blind through a stroke two days after the birth of her child. The case was so unusual that it was difficult to recognise and she had suffered as much from failure of diagnosis as from the condition itself. She was a charming patient and I heard from her regularly over the next twenty years – by which time she had very largely recovered her sight. My paper was not very important and has rarely been quoted but it was published and it was therefore on my CV. More importantly I learnt much about this rare form of blindness, how to investigate and diagnose it, and I was able to suggest the likely mechanisms that brought it about.

The need to publish sprang from the situation in the 1960s where too many doctors were available for too few jobs. Sadly the pressure on careers led, in some cases, to fraudulent publications where doctors made up results and deceived the profession and the public. I was the victim of such fraud but only realised several years after the

1. *Beryl Godwin-Austen (mother) and author*

2. Shalford Park House, Surrey

3. Papplewick Hall, Nottinghamshire

4. *Sir Henry Edmund Austen*

5. *General Sir Henry Thomas Godwin KCB*

6. *Robert Alfred Cloyne Godwin-Austen FRS*

7. *Maria Elizabeth Godwin-Austen (née Godwin)*

8. Mount Godwin-Austen (K2) from a painting by HHG-A 1861

9. General Sir A. Reade Godwin-Austen KCSI

event when the doctor in question was sent to prison! It happened like this.

When I was working as a Senior Registrar at the National Hospital, Queen Square, I was approached with the request to conduct an investigation into the use of a new drug for Parkinson's disease. I had already done some research in this field and had met most of the colleagues who were interested and had published on the subject. One individual had written much about this particular drug and its effects so my starting point was the place that he had reached. I set out the questions needing to be answered. I defined the methods of investigation to answer them and I began to assemble the results. It took more than a year to accumulate sufficient data but before I had done so this man published a paper covering exactly the same ground. I could not believe that he had worked so fast and I concluded that he must have access to funding and personnel that allowed him to gazump me in this way. My work was wasted and could not be published even though it reached conclusions different to his in many respects.

Only some five years later did I discover that he had made up his 'perfect' results and had taken several millions of pounds from a pharmaceutical company to 'fund the research'.

Although I embarked on a series of research projects with my future career in mind and with little or no ambition to make seriously important discoveries, the importance of research work in the life of practising physicians is considerable. As a student, learning medicine was an exercise in memory. After qualifying as a doctor the importance of human relationships was gradually appreciated. But it was several years before I realised that the knowledge I had acquired so laboriously had been gained by wise and conscientious men making careful observations, recording them and finally considering the implications for the better practice of medicine: in two words − clinical research. The result of clinical research in my lifetime has been twofold.

First it has led to enormous progress in the management of disease and through this the extension of life expectancy, much relief of suffering and the dramatic fall in infant mortality.[4] This progress has grown out of the application of extraordinary scientific discoveries especially in the field of pharmacology. In thirty years, death − from infection of the nervous system, from the complications of raised blood pressure (including stroke) and from epileptic convulsions – has become a rarity where formerly it was commonplace. And the management of neurological disability, especially for example in Parkinson's disease, has improved to the point where most patients can continue at work and are able to lead an active life. Most neurological disorders now have effective treatment available where thirty years ago the doctor was too often only able to make a diagnosis and provide limited symptomatic treatment. It is note-worthy that these real health improvements have resulted from the advances in science applied to the patient through medical research. The enormous investment in the administration and management of the Health Services has contributed practically nothing to these health improvements – indeed it has become evident that political and economic considerations are leading to a decline.

The second benefit from research activity has already been touched upon. To remain diligent, caring and competent in medicine a doctor must remain motivated. Clinical research requires awareness of what is not known, and the interest and enthusiasm to discover. At a personal level, motivation – to do your best for your patients – is often driven by the informed, enquiring mind of clinical research. And some of the decline of medical services can be attributed to the loss of commitment to research, observation and discovery.

The reader may find these thoughts at best hypothetical so I must return hastily to personal experience. I have found the research work that I have been involved in, exciting and motivating. Research is always collaborative and the shared enthusiasm and commitment is rewarding.

As a Senior Registrar at the National Hospital for Neurology, Queen Square, I developed a series of research projects into the medical treatment of Parkinson's disease and related disorders. This work led increasingly to the referral to me of patients with this condition so that within five years of being appointed Consultant in Nottingham I had more than four hundred patients with this disease whom I had seen and most of whom I was continuing to treat. Listening to these patients giving me their stories gave me an appreciation of the huge range of symptoms in this disorder and the extent to which patients' experience and suffering varies. Following patients over the years and observing how their illness evolved, I perceived that there were two distinct patterns of Parkinson's disease

– rather than the single form of the disease that had been described by James Parkinson in 1817. This observation affected management of the condition because patients with Type I Parkinson's disease responded to treatment differently to those with Type II. Those with Type II disease were much more likely to suffer mental problems so that their management and prognosis was different.

These observations led to fruitful collaboration with colleagues leading to a series of publications and the recognition of 'Diffuse Lewy Body Disease' (Type II Parkinson's). The work owed much to the inspired contribution of colleagues in neurochemistry and neuropathology in Nottingham, Professor R. J. Mayer and Professor J. Lowe, and has been carried forward with advances in knowledge in molecular biology to the development in animals of models of Type I and Type II Parkinson's disease. There is now (2006) for the first time a real prospect of developing treatments specific to each type. Such treatment would aim to arrest the condition from the time of diagnosis.

Although the aim of clinical research is always to improve the management of disease and thereby the suffering of the patient, clinical research also maintains motivation in the doctor and promotes the acquisition of knowledge both of which are essential for career progress.

When I was a registrar at the Maida Vale Hospital for Neurology and Neurosurgery I worked for the great Lord Brain. He attended for a ward round on Thursdays and afterwards, took tea with the ward sister. All the junior staff were expected to attend. Lord Brain (formerly Dr Russell Brain) had had a most distinguished career at the London Hospital (now the Royal London Hospital). But he was without humour and never indulged in any form of smalltalk. The Thursday tea parties were difficult because the junior staff had to provide conversation sufficiently intelligent to engage the great man. My junior colleagues at that time were Australian and lacked all sense of humility in the Presence; they were also relatively unaware of the nuances of social convention and conversation. After a prolonged silence during one excruciating tea party, Bob Crowe cleared his voice and said: 'Sir, to what do you attribute your greatness?'

Everyone apart from Lord Brain was horrified and we held our breath with embarrassment. We could think of no way to retrieve the situation, and silence descended again while his Lordship considered the question. Finally he replied: 'Whenever anyone has ever asked me to do something I have said "yes". And I have always taken Wednesday afternoons off.'

And that was all he said – honest, reticent, accurate and to the point. What he didn't say but was also true was that everything he had done he had done conscientiously and capably.

Lord Brain was part of the pre-War generation of neurologists; Elkington, and Kremer were also part of this generation. The next generation were men in their fifties who had mostly fought in the War, and were the controlling professional group at that time. Kelly and Gilliatt are names already mentioned for whom I had worked. When I was at the Maida Vale Hospital I worked for two consultants of the same era. Ronnie Henson had published important work on disorders of the nervous system associated with cancers. He was a small fussy man who patronised rather than teaching; and it seemed that he was never satisfied with my care of his patients. I could not respect him for his clinical skills, but I much admired his musical ability. He played the cello in a quintet, which met at his house every week. They were all up to professional standards. Henson also edited a major work on *The Neurology of Music*. This has remained the reference work on the subject.

My other consultant at the Maida Vale was John Marshall. It would be hard to think of someone more different from Ronnie Henson. Marshall was brisk, self confident, and very competent. He got through an enormous amount of work in outpatients and his patients loved him. He left me to manage his patients on the ward, going round only once a week, but telephoning me at 10 p.m. to ask how I was coping. I learnt much from John Marshall. But his personal life was kept private. He never entertained, I never met his wife and he never referred to any outside interests. He was Roman Catholic and once I tried to contact him in the evening to find that he was running a Catholic counselling service on Family Planning in a poor part of London. He had apparently been committed to this work for many years.

The Post-War generation of Neurologists were about ten years older than me. There had been a large number of appointments in the1960s. At that time the competition was intense and the quality of ability in this generation was very high. Roger Bannister, Ralph Ross-Russel, Ian McDonald and Michael Espir are names that will come into this story later.

Gilliatt and Kelly I have described as the 'controlling professional group'. I refer to the influence they had in the organisation of neurological postgraduate teaching and services. It is now almost unbelievable that consultants could impose their ideas about management on the structure of the NHS. For example, in London at that time there were two established specialist neurological hospitals – the Maida Vale, and Queen Square (formerly known as the 'Hospital for the Epileptic and Paralysed'). It seemed a good idea to amalgamate these hospitals thereby creating a 'National Hospitals for Nervous Diseases' group. There were advantages of scale, kudos, and influence nationally and internationally. The National Hospitals could speak for all neurologists in matters of policy, and in postgraduate education. Gilliatt and Kelly pushed forward this plan and achieved complete success. For thirty years British neurology was seen as pre-eminent and the National Hospitals were the flagship. Since the NHS reforms of the 90s such beneficent progress has become a thing of the past.

I worked at both hospitals as Registrar; then spent a year in pure research, working in neuro-physiology with Tom Sears. The aim of this work was to obtain the postgraduate degree of MD at London University; and the subject of my thesis was to elucidate the neurological basis of the symptom of shortness of breath. The five classical senses have been the subject of scientific, philosophical, and literary study since the dawn of civilisation, but shortness of breath (dyspnoea), while a common symptom in medicine, does not fit into the recognised senses of sight, smell, taste, hearing, or touch. After a years work I was able to conclude that position sense (related to touch) in the chest gives rise to this percept. The year also opened my eyes to the discipline of Basic Science and introduced me to the rarefied world of the Physiological Society. I was awarded my MD and was also given the Queen Square Prize for best work published at the National Hospitals in 1969.

I returned to clinical work, seeing patients, when I was appointed Senior Registrar to Outpatients at Queen Square. Neurology is mainly an outpatient specialty; my job was to see about thirty new referrals to the hospital each day, to make a diagnosis and sort them for referral and detailed assessment. It was admirable training for a consultant appointment, which was beginning to appear on my horizon.

CHAPTER 8

Britannia Road and Park Terrace

WHEN I MOVED TO QUEEN SQUARE, travel from Maida Vale became difficult and for some time we had wanted to invest in larger and more convenient accommodation. My mother lent us £4,000, and Jane and I searched for affordable housing somewhere on the Piccadilly Line. Eventually we found a derelict house in Fulham near the Moore Park Road and Fulham Broadway Underground. We bought the house with the £4,000, and then borrowed a similar sum to restore it. Electricity, gas, plumbing and heating had to be installed and for six months we lived in total squalor with two small children. The house was shrouded in scaffolding, and when things were really bad we decamped to Surrey to stay with my parents. After one such break, we returned to find that our bed had been slept in and, judging by the smell and grime, the intruder was a tramp. We could not secure the scaffolding, and spent the night terrified that at any moment the gentleman would return.

The job of supervising the workmen, arranging deliveries, and caring for the children kept Jane extremely busy. But we found that we had landed in a friendly and supportive neighbourhood. Next door were Charlie and Doll (Woolston), with two grandparents and one daughter. Charlie was a plumber and at weekends he and I fitted basins in the bedroom and radiators for the central heating. The street, Britannia Road, was a village in itself and over time we got to know everyone. Many remained firm friends after we moved to the Midlands.

It was therefore a considerable blow when, just as we had completed our restorations, the Labour Council announced that it planned to demolish all the houses in our area and build modern council flats.

Travelling on the Underground every day I had noticed a man of my age whom I knew to live about a hundred yards from our house. I decided to knock on his door and discuss with him whether there was a way of opposing the Council's plans. Peter Fane turned out to be just the right man for the project. Peter looked the typical City gent, with dark suit, polished shoes, bowler hat and rolled umbrella. He worked in insurance in the City, and had the mind of an efficient businessman and administrator. He also had a delightful sense of humour. He, Jane and I formed the 'Moore Park Road Residents Association'. Jane knocked on doors, collected signatures and support, and generated publicity and enthusiasm. Within a month, we had appointed a committee, which met every two weeks to decide how to plan our campaign and raise the necessary funds. The antique dealers in the New King's Road gave strong support because their businesses depended on our success.

At the appropriate time we demanded a Full Public Enquiry into the Redevelopment Plan. It was granted and we then had to raise the enormous sums necessary to commission an Expert Report and to pay Leading Counsel to put together our case for the Inspector. Sam Silkin QC (brother of the MP) accepted the brief, and in due course presented the case in front of the Inspector. It is interesting that in 1969, Counsel's fees for advice, preparation of the case and presentation over three days to the Inspector was only £3,000. Jane had done an enormous amount of preparatory work in the course of which she had met many of the officers at Fulham and Hammersmith Town Hall. When the Council elections came up she decided to stand, and in due course she was elected in a landslide for the Tories.

The Residents' Association won its case against the Council plans. There was relief at our success and much celebration. I still feel that we owed much of this success to Jane who had used charm, humour and hard work to achieve it. She remained on the Council for three years. It took much of her time in evening meetings but fortunately I was able to look after the children while she went out. She also had official duties and in spite of her smallness she developed a 'presence' and an attractive style. I was very proud of her.

The children changed from babies to small people at Britannia Road. Jonathan made friends that he has kept ever since. And Alice started dancing classes at Miss Vacani's School. This in turn led to her later successful, if short, career in ballet.

John Hughes had married the delightful Jen, and one day he rang to ask whether we would share a week at St Tropez with them. Alice was three, and Jonathan five. It was their first encounter with sand and seawater. The first morning we drove to the beach, and set up our 'patch' with rug, picnic, and towels. I settled down with a copy of *The Times* which I had managed to find in the town. The children played happily in the sand, and wandered off a short distance. Suddenly Alice came running back, 'Mummy, Mummy, there's a lady there with NO CLOTHES ON!! And she looks like ... a rubbish heap!'

At that moment the rest of the beach started to peel off all their clothes. We realised with alarm that we were on a nudist beach where the public were allowed to be naked from 11 a.m. I am afraid that we were cowards. We packed up and headed for the car to look for a more suitable beach.

Roger Gilliatt had emphasised in his characteristic forceful way that it was essential to be appointed Consultant before the age of thirty-five. 1970 became an ominous horizon for me as I worked my way through Registrar, Research Assistant and Senior Registrar jobs. My academic record was insufficient to move into a Research career and I had not developed a specialty interest outside clinical neurology (e.g. clinical neurophysiology). If I was unsuccessful at obtaining a Consultant appointment emigration was the only option.

One Sunday evening I was having supper with my friend and contemporary Michael Harrison. We had been on duty at the National Hospital, Queen Square over the weekend and inevitably the conversation revolved around our respective careers. Michael had worked as a General Medical SHO (Senior House Officer) in Oxford when Tony Mitchell was First Assistant to the redoubtable Professor George Pickering, Regius Professor of Medicine. Michael had expressed an interest in neurology and Tony Mitchell had suggested to him that if he became trained in neurology he, Dr Mitchell, would arrange a Consultant post for him. I already knew this background but Michael repeated it over Sunday supper because the promised job had just been advertised. Michael had managed to complete his training as promised and was looking forward to his appointment and to working again with his friend Dr, now Professor, Tony Mitchell. Our conversation then turned to my plans, and I expressed anxiety at facing appointments committees – something that I had only previously done for humble junior jobs.

'Why not gain experience by putting in an application for my job?' said Michael. 'After all, you will know that you aren't going to get it so you will have nothing to be nervous about.'

'But do you mind?'

'No, of course not.'

So we travelled by train together for the interview in Nottingham. I have a dim recollection of some hostile questioning from the Professor of Medicine – which seemed quite unnecessary. Michael was interviewed after me and there was then about an hour to wait. At last the Committee Secretary came into the waiting room and said the astonishing words: 'Dr Godwin-Austen, would you go and speak to the Chairman? Dr Harrison, please stay here.'

I suddenly realised that they had appointed *me*. I was appalled. I had stolen the job Michael had been promised. What would he do?

In a daze I went back into the boardroom. The Consultants who had interviewed me were now sitting smiling at me while the Chairman asked me to accept the job. Tony Mitchell was the first to shake my hand and to congratulate me. This was an act of great magnanimity because he had lost a major battle. I had been appointed Consultant Neurologist to the Nottingham and Derby Hospitals against his advice.

The background to my appointment was complicated but had nothing to do with my capabilities. This background gives some insight into the way our lives are so often shaped by unforeseeable events and personal ambition.

Dr (later Professor) Bryan Matthews was the Consultant Neurologist to the Derbyshire Royal Infirmary. He was an outstanding clinician who had developed a large practice and earned the greatest respect of his colleagues – from neurologists elsewhere, from the hospital where he worked and from the General Practitioners he served. A longstanding friend of Bryan Matthews was Professor Henry Miller, Professor of Neurology at Newcastle upon Tyne.

The Professor of Neurology at Oxford had just retired and his job was advertised. This was the second senior Chair in Neurology in the country and two consultants were vying for the post. They both had appointments at the National Hospital, Queen Square – an establishment that Henry Miller hated and resented. But both applicants were outstandingly well-suited for the job. Ralph Ross-Russell was a triple blue and had obtained first class Honours at Oxford, going on to work for Sir George Pickering and to publish seminal research into stroke. Ian McDonald had an equally outstanding University career in New Zealand followed by an impressive research contribution in Professor Gilliatt's Department.

Professor Henry Miller resented the notion that this plum Chair might go to someone from Queen Square and he set about persuading Bryan Matthews to apply. At the appointment the two Queen Square applicants divided the Committee and Bryan Matthews was appointed as the compromise candidate. He was most ambivalent about accepting the job. But the story did not end there.

The appointment of Bryan Matthews to Oxford created a vacancy in Derby. When he had been in Derby, Matthews provided neurological specialist cover for Nottingham. Michael Espir was Consultant Neurologist in Leicester but realised the job in Derby would benefit through the creation of the new Medical School in Nottingham. To work as Consultant Neurologist in a Teaching Hospital was a recognisable step up from a non-teaching hospital as Leicester then was. Michael Espir therefore applied for the job in Derby and in due course was appointed, the first 'Consultant Neurologist to the Nottingham and Derby Hospitals', in 1968. Immediately he set to work to create the second consultant neurological appointment but as the job description took shape he realised the need was for an appointment independent of the Department of Medicine and Tony Mitchell. It was through Michael Espir orchestrating support for my candidature over that of Tony Mitchell's candidate that led to my appointment to the post of second Consultant Neurologist to the Nottingham Teaching and Derby Hospitals in July 1970.

These complex medical politics were unknown to me when I stumbled out of the boardroom looking for a public telephone to report my extraordinary news to Jane. She had said goodbye that morning fully expecting me to return that evening with the same status as I had left.

My report: 'They've given me the job!' was followed by twenty seconds silence and then: 'Where is Nottingham?'

But we both rapidly realised that this was the most incredible stroke of good fortune, and that conclusion has withstood the test of time. The main burden of re-orientating our lives, however, fell to Jane. To plan my work schedule was relatively easy; to organise rehousing and new schools for the children in a part of the country which we knew nothing about was more difficult.

In the research work I did into the treatment of patients with Parkinson's disease, I had had the invaluable support of a junior colleague and friend, Christopher Frears. When he heard my news he told me that his father, Russell Frears, was a GP in Nottingham and immediately he arranged an introduction. Jane's first visit to Nottingham was therefore to meet Russell Frears. He turned out to be a most charming, cultured man as devoted to his patients as they were to him. He lived in a Regency terrace house, two hundred yards from the Nottingham General Hospital (where I was to work) in an area called 'The Park' which is unusual in being a residential development of large houses adjacent to the city centre. Our first question to Russell Frears was to ask where we should start our house-hunting. After a moment's thought he replied: 'Well, you could do worse than the house next door.'

It transpired, over our second glass of sherry, that the neighbour had just retired and bought a house in Derbyshire. The house was not yet on the market but Dr Frears suggested that the owner 'would probably accept an offer of £14,000'. We peered over the garden wall and saw a handsome Regency house with a large bay window looking south over a steeply-sloping, small garden. With its proximity to the hospital it seemed ideal. I bought a pad of writing paper and envelopes at the motorway service area and made the offer recommended. It was accepted by return! Our first problem was solved.

There was a sad sequel to this our first encounter with Frears senior. Russell Frears' first wife had borne him three children of whom Christopher was the youngest. But she died of a heart attack in her thirties. In retrospect her death was probably due to high fat levels in the bloodstream (familial hypercholesterolaemia). Christopher was a charming and generous man who had become an able and conscientious neurologist. He was appointed Consultant Neurologist in Plymouth but within six months he died, like his mother, of a heart attack leaving a wife and two children.

When we moved to Park Terrace, Nottingham, Jonathan was eight and down to start boarding at a prep school in Sussex in September. This was now clearly unsuitable. My old friend, Gillian Bird from medical student days, had married the delightful Neil Maitland and their older child, James, was the same age as Jonathan and due to start boarding school near Market Harborough in September. Maidwell Hall School was about one hour from Nottingham and therefore seemed the ideal school for Jonathan. With help from Gillian and Neil, an appointment was arranged for us to meet the headmaster, Alec Porch, before he and his family went off on their summer holiday. It was a baking hot day when we set out for Maidwell Hall, anxious to make a sufficiently good impression for Jonathan to be accepted at such short notice. There were five of us – parents, children and the dog, Titus. Jane had the foresight to pack some biscuits and orange juice to sustain the children on the return journey.

We parked in front of the school, which was a beautiful Jacobean house. It had been hot in the car on the way down so we left the windows open for Titus, who remained in the car while we were shown around. Mrs Porch then suggested we go to the private wing where she had set out tea for us, and Alice's eyes lit up at the suggestion. But when we entered their dining room, Titus was cringing in the corner with the guilty smile on his face that is so characteristic of a Dalmatian. He had jumped out of the car window, found the tea and demolished it all – sandwiches, biscuits and cakes. All we could do was to offer the few biscuits we had brought with us. Jonathan was accepted and Alice forgave Titus for depriving her of the tea, which would have been the only enjoyable part of her afternoon.

Alice's school was simple. Michael Espir's two daughters attended a girl's day school half a mile from our house and he and Patricia Espir recommended it strongly. So Alice started at Greenholme shortly after her sixth birthday.

It took nearly a year to sell our house in London. I became quite neurotic over the debt of the bridging loan. School fees, two cars and a family growing up seemed to leave me poorer than I had been as a Senior Registrar. In the long run I aimed to balance my finances by income from private practice, and the house we had bought allowed one floor to be converted to consulting room, secretary's office, records room and waiting room. Jane took on the considerable task of organising my private practice. She furnished and decorated the rooms, she interviewed and recruited a part-time secretary, she organised a medical records system, kept the accounts and organised the tax returns. On my consulting day (Tuesday afternoon) she worked as receptionist and throughout the week, day and night, she answered the telephone, made appointments and reassured patients. As the result of her devoted support my private practice did not encroach on my NHS work and my income gradually increased year

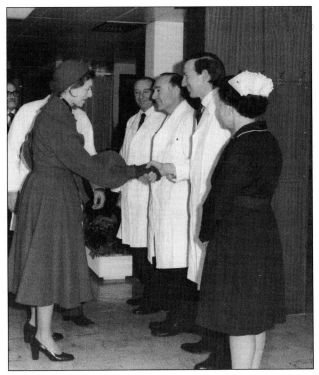

Princess Alexandra, QMC 1982. Julien Taylor, Michael Espir and self

on year. Without her assistance I would never have successfully established a private practice in Nottingham. The patients loved her and we began to feel a part of our new environment.

In order to further expand our finances, we decided to let the spare room in the attic. We gave it a coat of paint and bought some furniture at a nearby auction and after advertising locally we awaited a response. The first telephone call was a Mrs Grant, whose eighteen-year-old son needed a room near to the Playhouse Theatre in Nottingham where he was to spend a year as an actor with the company, earning his Equity card. In due course mother and son inspected the room and Jane made the arrangements and gave them tea. She reported to me: 'a delightful mother, and a shy and reticent son, who was *extremely good looking*, who hardly spoke a word.'

Hughie Grant (for it was the very successful actor) settled in well and stayed with us for the year. Like all actors he kept unconventional hours, and Jane was occasionally disturbed in the late morning to meet Hughie returning from a bath clad only in a towel wrapped loosely round his waist.

He had a motor scooter but found that it was not enough to get him up the motorway to visit his girlfriend in Leeds – a distance of some sixty miles. So Hughie developed the strategy of riding his scooter to the motorway, hiding it in some bushes near to the exit, and then thumbing a lift to Leeds. The plan worked well for several weeks but then the inevitable happened. One Sunday evening Hughie Grant was very late and we began to get worried. When he finally returned he had walked the five miles from the exit because his scooter had gone and was never seen again. However he persuaded the girlfriend to move to Nottingham. She was also a budding actress and in due course the two of them staged a show that they had written together. We were invited and felt somewhat out of place amongst all the 'luvvies'.

When I started in private practice I was entirely naïve about how patients were referred. But I quickly learned that the success of a private practice depends on getting known by the General Practitioners and by Consultant colleagues who refer the patients. In the hospital I met colleagues at lunch in the Consultants' dining room where cases were discussed, but it was more difficult to meet the GPs. Many of the best GPs used the NHS 'domiciliary consultation' to assess the qualities of the 'new neurologist'. I would be invited to meet the GP at the home of one of his neurological cases in the evening after work. The GP would introduce me to the patient and their problem, then weigh up the skill with which I related to the patient and the quality of the advice I gave. If I failed to come up to expectation, all referrals, both NHS and private, would go to Dr Espir or elsewhere (e.g. to London). The system had the advantage of encouraging best practice in every way – even down to the contemporary political obsession with waiting lists. Thus, if your waiting time for an out-patient appointment was judged by the GP to be unreasonably long in the clinical context of that patient's need, then the referral was to another clinic where the waiting time was shorter. The disadvantage of this system was that a minority of clinicians wanted to minimise their workload and referral rate –either because they did no private practice or because they lacked or had lost the motivation towards good clinical practice. Such lack of motivation was understandable and indeed justifiable where the individual's main interest and contribution was to research or teaching. But the system was certainly less costly, more efficient and more acceptable than one directed by politicians ('Waiting Times Directive' and 'Two Weeks Target')[5] or by lay administrators ('management').

CHAPTER 9

Isola and the Arabs

THE CHILDREN WERE GROWING UP and we became able to arrange more enterprising holidays. In 1971 we went camping in France and Italy towing a trailer containing a tent behind our little car. From a camping ground near Lake Garda we bought tickets for the opera in the Roman Arena at Verona. The production was *La Bohème*. Alice, aged barely seven, had been told the plot beforehand but was completely taken up by the story and the music. Mimi's death at the end of the opera finished her. As the final chord was played and in the momentary rest before the applause broke out a solitary wail of despair from Alice echoed around the Arena. The Italians loved it. They turned and applauded Alice for her sensitive reaction much to the embarrassment of her brother.

In 1973 we judged the children to be old enough to enjoy skiing and decided to go to the resort of Livigno. Our hotel was on the main nursery slope so when they were tired or cold they could take off their skis and go to their room in the hotel. Jane and I felt it was safe to leave them in the charge of their ski instructor while we went a short bus ride to the main ski lift. It was early January and the days were short. Jane and I came down the mountain late to find the bus had gone and we had a half hour walk through the twilight. Reaching our room we found both children tearful and wailing with distress. They had felt certain that some disaster had overtaken us; that their parents would never return; that they were alone in a foreign land and would be unable to get home. All very understandable emotions. Jane and I felt profoundly contrite and took the greatest care never to allow similar circumstances to occur again. It brought into focus the great blessing we had of two lovely and loving but vulnerable children.

In spite of this episode the skiing holiday in Livigno was a huge success. After we had returned to England, Jonathan one evening sought me out when I was doing some writing and said: 'May I talk to you about something, Daddy?'

With this opening I wondered what was to follow. But I put aside what I was doing and gave Jonathan my full attention. He had obviously prepared a little speech which went: 'Alice and I have decided that we don't want to go on summer holidays any more. Please can we always go skiing instead?'

How could I have refused, or even explain that skiing holidays were expensive? I solemnly took note of the request and was then exercised as to how to meet it.

About two months later I was idly reading the Sunday paper when my eye was caught by an advertisement.

'Why not enjoy a weekend in the Alps – skiing ABSOLUTELY FREE.' I scoured the small print – there seemed to be no catch – so we filled in the coupon and sent it off. Sure enough flight instructions and tickets duly arrived and we set off with a party of some twenty fellow travellers to Nice and thence by bus to the part-built new resort of Isola 2000.

Of course there was a catch. The builders (Bernard Sunley) wanted to sell the apartments they were building. Time-share hadn't been thought of but we were given a hard-sell after having experienced all the facilities and the setting. We were sufficiently impressed to conclude that an investment (mainly borrowed from the French State Mortgage Organisation) in a small apartment would satisfy the request

Skiing at Isola 2000

of the children and held the possibility of a wise investment. In fact it turned out to be the best investment I ever made.

Isola 2000 is situated next to the National Park of Mercantour at an altitude of 2,000 metres above sea level. In those days it had enviable snow and sunshine statistics and the ski slopes had been laid out most carefully to take every advantage of the terrain. We had twelve wonderful years of skiing for several weeks a year and often having summer holidays in the mountains as well. The children became more proficient on skis than their parents and we skied as a family.

One year Jonathan decided to recruit three (male) friends and go skiing from the flat and this had full parental approval. At the last minute one of the four dropped out which completely upset Jonathan's calculations of the financial arrangements, which of course they were sharing. In some desperation he telephoned from university to ask if I would fill the gap. Thus I found myself with three energetic and extremely competent skiers being taken down precipitous slopes that I would otherwise have avoided. After the first day I obtained a stopwatch and organised competitions for them down the worst slopes thereby avoiding an embarrassing display of cowardice. In the evenings the young men went off to nightclubs and I remained in the apartment. I had foreseen that this was likely to happen and had brought with me all the material necessary to write a small neurology textbook. I am happy to say that it remained in print for many years and the proceeds paid for more holidays than that one!

In earlier chapters mention has been made of the Royal College of Physicians of London and the important examination that it sets to gain Membership of the College. This examination is effectively a postgraduate degree in General Medicine (as opposed to General Surgery) and provides the gateway to Consultant appointments in the Medical Specialties. The examination has always charged high examination fees and it is to be assumed that the expenses of the College are, to a considerable extent, dependent on these fees. Foreign graduates from the old Commonwealth used to rely on success in the Membership examination to enable them to return to their native land and to go into practice with the qualification to practise General Medicine. Their examination fees made up a substantial part of the total income from this source. But the cost to the candidate was considerable, not only in fees for the examination but also in travelling, attending a training course and studying in London; and in general subsistence for perhaps as long as twelve months or even longer. In the 1970s there was a declining number of foreign students able or willing to bear these costs and it inevitably led to a reduced income to the College, which was the subject of intense discussion.

Iraq in those times owed much to the Medical Services set up by the British during the British Mandate following the First World War. The traditional career path to Medical Practice in Iraq was by obtaining Membership of the Royal College of Physicians (MRCP) as described above. When the numbers started to fall off the college advertised for British physicians to teach students so that they took the MRCP in Iraq at the University Hospital in Baghdad. The remuneration offered was enticing. I had not been in Nottingham long enough to prevent me taking time off to take up the offer and so, in January 1976, I found myself on my way to Baghdad for three months.

I was to stay at the 'Baghdad Hotel' at the College's expense and I was provided with a car and driver. When I checked in I was handed a letter addressed to me with the Royal Arms on the flap. It was an invitation to dinner at the Residence of the British Ambassador, in three days' time. I noticed with relief that the invitation gave a telephone number (a postal reply was unlikely to get there in time) so I dialled the number but could get no connection after repeated attempts. Eventually I decided to turn up anyway at the appointed time.

The door was opened by John Grahame himself and I launched into apologies and explanations as to why I had not sent a formal letter of acceptance. He waved away my remarks and then explained that they had been off the telephone for a week. The reason, he understood, was because the 'normal' telephone-bugging device had broken so they were cut off until it was mended!

My neighbour at dinner was a pleasant-looking Iraqi lady gynae-cologist. Although it was clear that she spoke good English, she responded with monosyllabic replies to questions, and refused to make a comment or state a view on any subject. I was nonplussed and after several attempts at conversation I gave up and spoke only to my neighbour on the other side. At the end of the evening as we were preparing to leave, John Grahame asked this lady whether she might be able to give me a lift back to the Baghdad Hotel as it was on her way home. She readily agreed. As soon as we set off she started to talk, answering some of the questions I had asked earlier and giving definite views on local politics and personalities. At last there was a moment when I could ask her tentatively why she had not spoken like this earlier.

'Because all the Embassy buildings are bugged and I, an Iraqi, would be arrested if the authorities knew that I was a guest of the British Ambassador.'

The gradual acceptance of the loss of freedom that one suffers while living in a police state passes through several phases. The first is a sense of outrage and irritable resentment. This is followed by nervous, not to say frightened behaviour, which restricts conversation and limited me to doing my daily work and preventing me from going out or taking any interest in the country where I was. The Iraqis I met were invariably kind, intelligent, well-educated people. They were embarrassed to discuss politics and I believe frightened, so the final stage is acceptance of the status quo, while keeping one's thoughts to oneself.

I was in Iraq at a time when Saddam Hussein had established his dominance by executing the opposition, often by his own hand. The Kazzar plot to seize power had been put down with the execution of Nadhim Kazzar in 1973. After this incident and the Yom Kippur war, Saddam pursued a policy of ruthless suppression of opposition internally, and alliance with the Palestinians against Israel and her allies externally. Palestinian terrorists were given safe haven in Iraq, Abu Nidal and Wadi Haddad were believed to be living in Baghdad and organising anti-Zionist terrorism when I was there. All political demonstration was banned and there was a rumour, also while I was there, that three hundred Shias had been shot in the holy city of Kerbala for disobeying this rule and marching in a peaceful religious demonstration.

But Iraq is a fascinating country with a remarkable ancient history and many important archaeological sites including Babylon, Nimrud, Nineveh and Ur of the Chaldees. I had also read Wilfred Thesiger's description of the 'Marsh Arabs' in southern Iraq and at weekends hoped to be able to visit some of these places.

My contract to teach neurology included one visit from my wife. My period in Iraq was the first time we had been apart in fifteen years of marriage. The separation was hard to bear. One realised how much of the relationship one took for granted and I had time to analyse all the lovable qualities that Jane had. I therefore looked forward to her visit with considerable anticipation and laid plans to travel to the south with her the one week she was over.

The plan was to go by train to Nassiriyah, then take a taxi to Ur – a distance of about 25 miles. We could spend about two hours exploring the 1920–22 excavations of Sir John Wooley (artefacts from which are displayed in the British Museum in London). We were then to spend the night in the Rest House in Nassiriyah and on the Sunday be taken by car then boat around the Marshes including the island 'capital' – Chebayish. Finally we would return by train to Baghdad at around sunset.

The train journey was slow and hot. We had been warned to take food but no alcohol. An armed soldier stood at the end of every carriage and I began to feel a little uneasy about what we were letting ourselves in for. We reached Ur without mishap. The taxi driver spoke only Arabic but eventually understood where we wanted to go. Clearly there was little demand for tourist travel and when we reached Ur it was completely deserted. There were no visitors' facilities or charges. Only a handful of labels in Arabic and English marked the main sites, especially the tomb where the King was buried with the two hundred maidens who were sacrificed at the same time. I had read that skeletal remains of these maidens indicated that they were dressed in identical costumes containing gold thread and with their hair tied with identical ribbons. One girl had not had time to tie her hair before execution and the ribbon was still in her right hand five thousand years later.

While we were exploring Ur we were surprised to see a car approaching over the dead-flat desert. When a young couple got out it was clear they were Westerners and we went over and spoke to them. It turned out that they were from the American Embassy in Kuwait and were on their way driving to Baghdad. They were planning to reach Baghdad that night. I explained that the journey was more than two hundred miles, it was after 6.00 p.m. and on Iraqi roads they would be lucky to get there before midnight. We knew there was another double room in the rest house so I suggested that they follow our taxi and stay there for the night.

It was impossible to explain to the taxi man but I did not pay any attention to his nervousness at being followed back into town. We

came down to breakfast next morning and the Americans had
obviously left early. As we were sitting eating our breakfast two
enormous black-suited, criminal-looking characters entered the room
and sat down in the two vacant chairs at our table. They fixed their
gaze on me and said: 'You Zionist spy – you meet American Zionist
spy.'

The taxi man had reported us and in a flash I realised that we were
in an extremely dangerous situation. I tried to explain that I had a
contract with the Iraqi government to teach at the Medinah Hospital
in Baghdad. I produced our passports – the only official documents I
had with us – all to no avail.

'You are arrest.'

'But what are you going to do with us?'

After a short discussion between the two brutish-looking men, one
replied: 'We take you to the border Kuwait and give you to them
for prison.'

As Jane and I were taken out to the black Mercedes parked outside
the hotel, I had a brainwave.

The evening before we had set out on our journey, I had met an
Arab doctor friend in the bar for a drink before supper. I told him
our plans and he looked a bit worried. When I asked why he
explained that Nassiriyah was a very primitive place where we would
not find anyone who would understand English. And then he
remembered that he had met an Iraqi from Nassiriyah when they
were both training in London some years before. His friend was now
a qualified dentist and he knew his address in Nassiriyah. He wrote
the name and address on a scrap of paper but before putting it in my
pocket I made him write it out again in Arabic.

With some difficulty, standing outside the hotel, beside the
Mercedes, I told the 'heavy mob' that I had a friend who could
explain; and I gave them the Arabic version and asked to be taken
there. With some reluctance they agreed. Jane and I were squeezed
into the back of the car with the enormous black-suited gentleman
between us. When we arrived at the dentist's house he was saying his
prayers in front of the television so we all stood in silence around the
walls between our arresters until he finished. I gave him my name
and in fluent English he said: 'Of course, my friend telephoned last
night from Baghdad and said you might be coming. But who are the
people with you?'

I explained as briefly as I could that we were arrested as Israeli spies and were being taken to Kuwait for imprisonment.

There was then a prolonged exchange between the three and gradually it seemed that the heavy mob were explaining why they had acted as they had. Finally a deal was agreed. The two big men would stay with us all day and put us on the train to Baghdad that evening. There was no further mention of Kuwait. And so it was. We were driven to the little motorboat we had hired. The heavy mob sat together at the back so that the boat settled low in the water with its prow in the air and off we chugged to Chebayish.

There were flocks of pelicans, cranes, egrets, herons, duck and geese in an endless landscape of water and rushes. Out boatman found his way through narrow passages in the reeds. We passed the occasional characteristic reed hut housing one family with the buffalo and a goat on an island made of reed mats and measuring about 20 feet square.

At last we came to Chebayish which consisted of a cluster of man-made islands with some eight or ten reed huts standing on them, and that was nearly all that the Capital of the Marshes consisted of. But in the middle, looking completely out of place, was a lamp standard with an electric bulb burning in it. My inevitable first question was to ask how they had a street lamp in this tiny village way out in the Marshes. We were led to a miniature grass hut about three feet high and inside there was an old diesel generator. The attendant was sitting beside it with his oilcan and on top of the machine was stamped the maker's name: 'Rushton & Hornsby, Lincoln, 1929'.

We returned with our hostile guards to the rest house to pick up our luggage and we gave them a firm farewell as we got onto our train. We had narrowly avoided a possible 'disappearance' as Israeli spies.

Since this experience everything I have learnt has strengthened me in the belief that Saddam's Iraq was an intolerably brutal regime imposed on a country that never deserved him. It is a sad paradox that since the Iraq War liberal minded people in the west have sided with the 'Jihadists' and Ba'ath terrorists against Western forces that overthrew Saddam's fascist regime. The genocide terrorists increasingly (2007) causing civil war in Iraq can only lead to a state of murderous anarchy in a country which had the potential to be an educated, prosperous, peace-loving nation. Is there a solution?

Writing in 2007 my formula would involve first sealing the borders with Iran and Syria with the use of American and British forces; then assisting the Iraqi authorities to purge the National Police and Armed Services of Shia and al-Qaeda-Sunni insurgents; and finally progressively withdrawing Western forces from the country while maintaining rigorous control of the borders and leaving the good people of Iraq to rebuild their civilised country with Western aid. But perhaps it is already too late.

But I must return to 1976–77 and Saddam's regime that I experienced at first hand.

I had been given an admirable Sunday lunch by a doctor married to an Irish girl, and I learnt something of the loneliness of her position in a country she loved. The lunch had been delicious lamb stewed with *chimmah*. This is a form of truffle, which grows in the desert for a few weeks in the warm, rainy season in March. (It is probably the 'manna' mentioned in the Old Testament.)

I returned to my room in the Baghdad hotel to find the telephone in my room ringing continuously. When I lifted the receiver an angry voice said: 'I am the Minister of Health; you are to see the President. I take you now to the Palace.'

It was not for me to ask questions. I quickly changed into a suit and went downstairs. In the entrance hall of the hotel was a little, round man, pacing up and down. Outside were two large, black Mercedes and a fleet of six uniformed motorcycle outriders. As I was taken to the front Mercedes the Minister murmured: 'We do not talk in this car – it is bugged.'

We set off at speed with motorcycle sirens wailing, the traffic clearing itself out of the way. The Mercedes behind us was to prevent the strategy adopted by Saddam Hussein in the attempted assassination of Qassem in 1959. From the pillion of a motorcycle Saddam had been driven up behind the car in which Abdul Karim Qassem was travelling and shot him through the back window. Fortunately Qassem recovered from his wounds[6] but was executed in 1963 by Ahmad Hassan al-Bakr – the President of Iraq whom I was now being driven to see in medical consultation.

We turned into the entrance to the Presidential Palace where there were road barriers across our path.

'Here we get out and change cars,' said the Minister. As I got out of the car I asked him why this was necessary.

'Because there may be a bomb under,' was his surprising explanation.

We got into yet another black Mercedes on the far side of the barriers and were driven half a mile to the front of the Presidential Palace. This was a low, modest building set in woodland in a bend of the river Tigris.

I was sat in a drawing room containing gilded and very 'kitsch' furniture and a magnificent huge silk carpet. Within a few minutes President Bakr entered the room.

Ahmad Hassan al-Bakr was established President with the support of Saddam Hussein in 1968 after Bakr had organised a successful plot to overthrow President Arif. During his early years in office, also with the support of Saddam, Bakr had organised purges of 'spies' – mainly innocent Jews – who were hanged in Liberation Square in Baghdad. In 1976 the British Ambassador still referred to the square as 'the Hanging Gardens of Baghdad'. Gradually Saddam had taken over from Bakr in all the important decisions in the presidency. Two years before I saw him Bakr was said to have suffered a small stroke,[7] but the story he gave me was one of gradually increasing numbness in his hands and feet. He was an insulin-dependent diabetic and the signs on examination supported the conclusion that his complaints were due to diabetic neuropathy. Before I could make any pronouncements I was told that the Iraqi specialists who had seen the President were waiting to discuss the case in another room. When I went through there were no fewer than eleven physicians waiting, some of whom I already knew. They were understandably slightly resentful of a foreigner being called in. I explained my conclusions but the group became nervous. They, collectively (because there is safety in numbers), had told the President his symptoms came from arthritis of the spine in his neck. I explained the reasons why I favoured an alternative diagnosis and they emphasised the serious consequences of their diagnosis being wrong – banishment to General Practice in a remote village at best; removal from the Medical Register and even imprisonment at worst. So both diagnoses had to be agreed and I would arrange measurements of the nerve conduction velocity in a clinic in the hospital where I had assisted. But when I suggested the President should attend in the department at a time of his own convenience it was pointed out that if the President was known to be ill there might be a Revolution! So the equipment must come to the palace.

So it was, in the middle of the night, a platoon of soldiers loaded the wardrobe-sized EMG machine onto an Army lorry and unloaded it in the President's drawing room. At 7 a.m. I was taken to the palace (no outriders this time) to set up the machine and to do the test.

The Baghdad University Hospital EMG machine must have been bought – probably second-hand – in about 1960. It relied on glass valves rather than transistors and valves heated up and had to be cooled with a ventilation fan. During the transport the soldiers must have dropped the machine, bending the metal cabinet. When I switched on, the fan rattled loudly against the deformed cabinet. So I had to take out my screwdriver and remove all the outer casing. I think that the President was very impressed by all the valves visible and glowing red.

The diagnosis was confirmed and treatment advised to the apparent satisfaction of all. However, I later learnt that three months after this episode a medical team from George Washington University had been summoned at huge expense to treat the President. I was not even paid a fee!

In spite of declining health, Bakr remained President until 1979. All his titles and privileges were first removed by Saddam, who then replaced him. It is probable that he was murdered in 1982 at the command of Saddam Hussein by a team of doctors with a fatal dose of insulin injection.[8]

In spite of these ghastly atrocities I have never lost my respect for Iraq and for the Arabs. This was reinforced a few years later when I travelled to Saudi Arabia to give medical advice. It happened like this:

One evening ten days before Easter, Jane's cousin Dr Meyrick Emrys Roberts rang up. Meyrick had recently retired from General Practice and an old patient had asked him for the name of a neurologist who would be prepared to see a patient in the King Faisal Hospital in Riyadh. The patient was eighteen years old and had suffered a very severe head injury in a car accident. I was told that he was unconscious on Intensive Care.

I was not on duty for Easter so I accepted to travel Friday morning to Monday evening. Meyrick passed this on to the family and the brother of the patient then rang to explain the travel details. These included a man on a motorcycle collecting my passport for a visa; and I stopped off on my way to Heathrow at a house in Harlesden (not an area with which I was familiar) to retrieve my passport-with-visa, and to pick up my first class air tickets.

The only time I have ever travelled first class in an aeroplane was on this flight to Riyadh. As I sank into the enormous seat I requested a glass of champagne. Imagine my consternation at being told that Saudi Arabian Airlines is dry and it was 'soft drinks only'. As I waited for take-off I nursed my disappointment. At the last moment before the doors shut my neighbour in the next seat hurried on board with a large zip bag. He immediately opened it to reveal a bottle of champagne, which he generously shared with me.

The next morning I attended at the King Faisal Hospital and discovered that a friend and near-contemporary of mine at St Thomas's, David Barkham (later OBE), was Senior Physician and Superintendent of the hospital. As a result I was asked to see three other patients! But my patient in Intensive Care was obviously very severely head-injured. He was deeply unconscious but all the investigations indicated a brain-stem injury from which he was likely not only to survive but also to be capable of significant improvement.

That afternoon I met the family in their enormous house to discuss the case. In front of me was a low table with camphor-wood smouldering on a tray. All the male members of the family were sitting around the room. I was sat down on a low sofa along the wall. Behind the sofa was a perforated wooden screen over a large opening into the adjacent room, which was in total darkness. The female members of the family could be heard murmuring behind the screen from where they could listen to what I had to say.

I presented my opinion most cautiously. I was aware that if complications set in he might die. But if everything went well he might recover consciousness and then show improvement. When I had finished one of the brothers asked: 'When he wake up?'

I explained that it was very difficult to calculate when that would be and it was possible that he could remain permanently in a persistent vegetative state. They were obviously not happy with this explanation and eventually I said something like: 'If he does wake up it is likely to be after about six months.'

What I did not know was that after I left, the brothers got out their diaries and marked the exact date six months ahead. The oldest brother Sirhan Sirhan offered to show me Riyadh that afternoon and we set off in his open sports car with me clutching my precious camera. His first question was: 'What would you like as a present from the Sirhan family — you choose.'

Of course I was entirely confused as to what I should suggest. It was like a rich cousin from abroad asking a child what they would like for Christmas. I remembered the rule that Jane applied in these circumstances — always suggest something that was ephemeral and not permanent; and not too expensive. And I thought back to the lunch in Baghdad the day I saw the President.

'I would like some *chimmah* to take to my wife.'

Sirhan Sirhan was most impressed by my sophisticated choice and we headed off towards the market. When we got out of the car my camera was on the backseat with the hood down. I was nervous it might be stolen but my host dismissed the suggestion. When we returned twenty minutes later with a large bag of *chimmah*, the camera was where I had left it in full view of the market crowd milling around the car. I asked Sirhan how it was that no-one had been tempted to take my expensive camera.

'Because if they did their hand would be chopped off,' was the immediate reply.

The conversation then turned to other aspects of Sharia Law. The commonest crime in Riyadh at that time was by children taking unlocked cars and driving them away for joy-riding. I could not think of an appropriate limb to amputate for this crime so I asked what the penalty was.

'We put them in prison,' he replied.

'But what if the child is too young?' I said.

'Well that is a problem because we have children as young as five or six years old — sometimes two children — one standing on the seat to steer, the other on the floor operating the pedals! And in that case we send the children to prison with their father. Usually they are in prison only for two or three days but the father suffers for not supervising his child and he misses time from work, and for the child it seems like three months.'

On the Sunday before I flew back, David Barkham and his wife had invited me to lunch. He had had an interesting career since qualification. Because he had a large family to educate in England, he had taken the job in Uganda which included acting as personal physician to President Idi Amin. The situation in that country deteriorated and one day driving to work David saw a huge newspaper headline:

PRESIDENT'S PHYSICIAN
COMMITS POLITICAL
GONORRHOEA

He drove home, packed a suitcase, left for the airport and flew back to England the same day.

Finding another job had been difficult when he couldn't get a reference from Amin. He eventually secured the appointment in Saudi Arabia, and it was ironic that some years later Idi Amin fled to Saudi Arabia. David did not look him up.

We spent a very pleasant afternoon talking of the beauty of the Arabian desert especially in the spring, and the book that his wife was writing on the subject. Later they took me to the airport for my return journey.

There was a sequel to this episode. I was very busy in my outpatient clinic six months later. The telephone rang and it was Sirhan Sirhan.

'How are you, doctor?'

About ten minutes later the formalities were over but by that time my impatience was at breaking point.

'You remember Mohammed, my brother who is sick? He wake up when you say. The six months after you see him we make a party to celebrate – and he wake up!'

As in Nassiriyah my guardian angel had been watching over me. I arranged for Mohammed to be brought to England and admitted to the private wing for intensive physiotherapy and rehabilitation. He did very well and was walking and feeding himself three months later when he returned to Saudi Arabia and to the care of his lovely family. A further six months and I heard that Mohammed had returned to University.

CHAPTER 10

Papplewick Hall

IT WAS THE LATE 1970s, and I was driving home to Nottingham through the village of Papplewick. As I approached the village a most spectacular view opened to my right. Over a low stone wall I could see a field sloping gently away to the west. About 200 yards down the slope, which was dotted with carefully placed trees, was a large yellow stone house with a curved wall connecting it to what seemed to be a stable block. The house had classical proportions, and the details of the façade clearly identified it as eighteenth century – in the style of Robert Adam.

Beyond the house the park sloped down between higher ground planted with Scots pine on one side and chestnut and beech on the other. In the middle distance the village church tower, punctuated the view before a shallow wooded river valley. The ground then rose slowly through fields and hedgerows until an unspoilt view ended some five miles away at a range of hills, which I later learnt had the unusual name of the 'Misk Hills'.

I got out of my car and watched the sun set over this Arcadian English landscape. And when I reached Park Terrace, I told Jane what I had seen.

'If ever we move from here there is only one house I would prefer to this and it is called Papplewick Hall.'

From that time I started to make enquiries about Papplewick Hall and its owner. I quickly learnt that it was unlikely to come on the market, and anyway it was large, unheated, inconvenient and unsuitable for a modern, middle-aged, middle-class couple with two teenage children. But I couldn't suppress my interest.

Claude Chadburn and his wife Ethel had bought the Hall in the early 1930s, along with a four thousand-acre estate, with cottages, farms, a cricket ground and the church livings. Claude Chadburn was then managing director of Mansfield Brewery. In the recession, brewers were some of the few who continued to run a successful business and as he prospered Claude did much to restore the house and improve the land. His five children were brought up at Papplewick and until the outbreak of war in 1939 the future looked promising.

He laid out the estate for pheasant and partridge shooting and complained much how the birds were ruthlessly poached. There was a horse trial course laid out in the park and a cricket ground created by the Old Dairy (later the pavilion). In the late 60s, Claude still employed a butler. On one of his shooting days, John Radford remonstrated, 'Claude, why on earth do you still have a butler?'

To which Claude had replied, 'But who else is to answer the telephone?'

To the end of his life Claude and Ethel Chadburn maintained a standard of living reminiscent of the Edwardian era. Potted palms graced the drawing room, and in winter the living room was heated only with open fires. The kitchen was down six steps at the other end of the house from the spacious and elegant dining room.

There were two sons and three daughters. Both sons went away to the war. The elder son was killed in North Africa at Knightsbridge and within the year the younger son was killed on a motorcycle half a mile from Papplewick Hall. Claude's hopes for the estate and his family appeared to be shattered. But more was to come.

All three daughters married. The oldest (Joyce) had a son (Anthony Cundy) who took up farming and was given 'Top Farm' on the estate by his grandfather.

The youngest daughter, Anne, married a farmer on the estate, David Weston. Everyone I have spoken to has said what a nice man David Weston was, and it is likely that Claude planned for the inheritance of the estate to pass to David Weston, but it was not to be.

When Claude was in his seventies, the South Notts Hunt had the usual meet at Papplewick and assembled in front of the Hall. David Weston suddenly and for no obvious reason fell from his horse and hit his head. He died a few hours later. Once again Claude's hopes for the future seemed to be shattered. But by this time Anthony Cundy was proving to be an extremely capable farmer. At some point Anthony was promised the inheritance of the Hall and this probably led to the rumour I heard that it was not likely to come on to the market. But again, Claude's hopes and plans did not come to pass.

By 1970 Claude Chadburn was an old man. The maintenance of a large historic house and the management of the estate were responsibilities that he must have found to be increasingly onerous. He was persuaded to set up a Trust for the benefit of his remaining children. The Hall would be part of the Trust and Mr and Mrs Chadburn would live in the Hall paying rent to the Trust. Maintenance of the house would be carried out by the Works Department of Mansfield Brewery. These arrangements, while convenient for Claude, and probably most tax efficient, took away from him the right to decide who inherited the estate. It also meant that repairs to the roof, stonework and lead guttering were carried out by Brewery builders, who had no knowledge or sympathy for an eighteenth century building which was, by then, Grade 1 listed.

Claude Chadburn died in 1977, and his widow Ethel in 1982. The Trust for the house and estate decided to sell, thus disappointing Anthony Cundy, who had expected to inherit the house. It was put up for auction. At this point I had the wild idea of trying to buy it. There were six weeks before the auction date. I arranged the usual searches and survey and incurred significant expense, and then three weeks before the auction a letter arrived to say that the Trust had decided to accept an offer prior to auction and the house was no longer available. Enquiries revealed that an offer of £300,000 for the estate, including the house, farmland, cottages and cricket ground, had been received from Ernest Ottewell. Within three months Ottewell had carved the estate up into smaller parcels, sold the land and reputedly had doubled his money. We were disappointed, but also relieved to think we had been saved the responsibility.

It was the autumn of 1982, Jane was approaching her forty-fifth birthday and we decided to spend some of the funds accumulated for the purpose of Papplewick Hall on a birthday celebration. At that time Cunard were offering a special package by their flagship the QE2 sailing to New York, flying back on Concorde. The QE2 was the most prestigious and luxurious vessel afloat; and Concorde was the unique supersonic passenger aircraft. The trip to New York was an indulgence and an opportunity to sample the pinnacle of British engineering achievement.

We arrived at Southampton on a cold day in early November. As we went up the gangplank a Guards Band was playing military marches on the quay. Jane was wearing a fur coat. I was in my best grey overcoat. We looked a handsome couple and it was probably for this reason that we were offered places on the Captain's table in the dining room. Our cabin was the cheapest available. The rest of the Captain's table were all in expensive outside state rooms, but they were sociable and interesting people. Among them was a single most attractive American lady of our age. Jane Denison became a close friend of my Jane's. She was full of fun and enthusiasm. She worked as a journalist on the *Washington Post* and although she never mentioned it until much later, Jane Denison had been working at the *Washington Post* on the scandal of the Watergate break-in, which led to Nixon's impeachment some years later.

Jane Denison's mother was a Kendrew, which was the maiden name of our friend Marcia Abel Smith. We later gave a dinner party for the Kendrews at which Marcia, her brother Tim, their father General Sir Douglas Kendrew and his wife Lady Kendrew, Jane Denison, and her cousin, Edwin Kendrew (who was the architect responsible for the restoration of Williamsburg), were all present. It proved to be the last large dinner party that we gave at 12 Park Terrace.

Our four days on the *QE2* passed in a haze of fine eating, interesting new friendships, parties and dancing till the early hours to big band music of Glenn Miller. We felt young again; it was like a second honeymoon.

The arrival in New York coincided with sunrise over Manhattan. The enormous ship berthed on the west side and the journey to the Waldorf Astoria took about five minutes. We sampled a helicopter ride over New York to complete our experience of twentieth century technology, and we went to the theatre and visited friends.

The journey home was a remarkable experience. *Concorde* had been flying for only a few years, but British Airways had earned a reputation for the ultimate in luxurious air travel. The journey to Kennedy airport was taken in a 'stretch limo'. Our luggage was not seen again until Heathrow. We walked on a red carpet to the Concorde departure lounge where there were copies of *The Times* for that day (it was about mid-day). Our overcoats were removed and returned as we left the plane in London.

The plane was parked outside the windows of the departure lounge but it seemed much smaller as we boarded. Two seats each side of the aisle and perhaps fifteen rows — more like a bus than the 'jumbos' we have since got used to. The speed was displayed on a 'Machmeter' at the front of the cabin. We went through the sound barrier over Nova Scotia. The Machmeter registered 1.0 and the noise of the engines dropped so the cabin was curiously quiet. But the windows were warm and the earth could be seen far below as a sphere, with the shadow from the sun moving slowly across from the east. We were served lunch/supper on *Concorde* and the place setting was with beautiful Waterford cut crystal glasses inscribed with a crown above a capital C. At a convenient moment, I asked the cabin steward whether it would be possible to buy a set of glasses. I saw him discussing this request with the head steward, who then approached me to apologise that they were not permitted to do this. I readily accepted the ruling, but I was surprised as we were leaving the plane. The head steward thrust a brown package into my hands. And of course later inspection showed it to contain the six Concorde wineglasses.

About a year later I received a telephone call from someone who had bought Papplewick Hall from Ernest Ottewell. Her name was Mrs James. She had been widowed when her husband. a dentist. had died unexpectedly and she had decided to create employment for herself, hoping to convert Papplewick Hall into a nursing home. But Gedling Council would not give permission for the conversion and she had decided to sell.

'Are you still interested in buying the Hall?'

'What price are you asking?'

She named a figure far higher than I was prepared to pay. When I said what price I was prepared to pay she exploded with anger and put the telephone down. I forgot about this call and made no further enquiries.

Six months later, she telephoned again. The asking price had come down but otherwise the conversation was as before. Twice more, she rang at about six month intervals; by now, it was mid-1985, and the Hall had been empty for two winters. When she phoned the fourth time indicating Papplewick Hall was still unsold, I was peremptory.

'I will give you £120,000 only. If you don't accept this offer within two weeks please never telephone me again.'

A letter accepting my price arrived a week later; the price was less than half what she had asked originally. But just what had we let ourselves in for?

The lead gutter on the south front had collapsed, allowing the rain on that quarter of the roof to wash down the inside of the wall. It had carried away about one third of the beautiful plasterwork ceiling in the dining room. In every room was something similar. Mansfield

Brewery works department had patched rather than mending in Claude Chadburn's day. Major restoration was now necessary.

Jane however had always been enthusiastic about taking on this work. So we set a date for the move on 27 February 1986. And Jane started with a survey of the work necessary and then set about finding the appropriate craftsmen.

Seven weeks before we moved Jonathan suffered a very severe fracture of his femur while skiing. Hospital treatment in France and in Nottingham led to the announcement that he would be off traction and ready to come home on 28 February – the day set aside to move into Papplewick. We persuaded the hospital to keep him an extra day and then Jonathan was carried up to the top floor bedroom where he stayed for a further six weeks until he was able to bear some weight on the leg that had been broken.

This was not the only crisis at that time. A cold spell of weather had kept the temperatures below freezing from about ten days before the move. The main water pipe was frozen so no water was coming into the house. There were several burst pipes and all the lavatory bowls had burst, except one. The first day was spent with me assisting two plumbers with blowtorches unfreezing and repairing pipework and lavatory pans; while Jane, wearing all the clothes she could muster, was stoking fires, plying us with hot drinks and supervising the installation by a friend, George Nall, of a magnificent Scandinavian wood burning stove.

Jane had already realised that it was essential to move the kitchen from the north wing into the old morning room in the main house. This needed planning permission. Jane did only minimal cooking in the old kitchen because she realised that if the local authority knew we could manage with the old kitchen (twenty yards and six steps away from the dining room) they would never give permission.

For three months, we waited for planning permission to be granted. Jane called weekly on the planning department at Gedling, and she got to know all the officers involved. But during those three months, she cooked on a microwave and a 'Baby Belling' electric stove, and we washed up in a bucket filled with water from an electric kettle.

The main immediate restoration was to the outside – the roof, the lead guttering, the stonework, joinery and paintwork. We found expert craftsmen in these trades and recruited them as individuals with agreed rates of pay. They each surveyed the work to be done and gave figures for the number of hours they needed. Scaffolding would be necessary over the whole house and this would be a major expense. If we were efficient, the work could be done in sixty-five days. We hired the scaffolding for seventy days and told each member of the team the date when the scaffolding would come down.

Each evening, when I got back from work, Jane and I climbed the scaffolding and inspected the work done. Each morning, Jane, the 'foreman and works manager', climbed the scaffolding and gave the instructions to the workforce. The ten men all worked magnificently. Jane and I became experts in Georgian house construction with my specialty being lead-work guttering.

On the seventieth day the scaffolding men arrived. The slates were on and the guttering was finished. But the day previous the stonemasons had been finishing off the stonework repair, creating dust and thereby preventing the painters covering the new window joinery as the scaffolding came down. The painters did the top floor windows and agreed to finish the lower windows from long ladders.

The park and garden of Papplewick Hall had been laid out as landscape and woodland in the eighteenth century. In the three summers that the Hall had been empty, it had become completely overgrown. Grass and brambles were waist high and fallen branches blocked the paths. The main flowerbed had disappeared completely. I therefore needed to buy some heavy equipment and aim to resuscitate the main lawn through the summer and the woodland during the first winter. Finally, the interior was restored as funds became available and this process was spread out over ten years.

When we gave our first party to celebrate the bicentenary of Papplewick Hall in 1987, the dining room plasterwork was just complete and the main hall was finished. The ceiling of the hall is forty feet above a stone floor. The painters, Ben Smith and Steve, were devoted to Jane. She wanted a pale blue ceiling in the hall. A construction of ladders, trestles and planks was erected to reach the ceiling. Strong lining paper was applied and the paint mixed and approved. When we saw the result, we immediately exclaimed the colour was too strong. I was for not asking for a repaint. It was too dangerous at the top of rickety planking. But Jane was determined everything must be right. The next day Ben took the news calmly and within the hour Jane had her perfect blue ceiling.

Welcome to the Bicentenary Party, 1987

The Bicentenary Ball was masked Fancy Dress, in the costume of the eighteenth century – contemporary with the house. Alice recruited a team of 'serving wenches' dressed appropriately, and they controlled a buffet of eighteenth century food. Jonathan gathered a group of footmen for car park duty and drink serving. We were unable to find the necessary number of footmen's costumes, so they were colourfully dressed in Beefeater costume, normally used in Gilbert and Sullivan productions. Jane made herself a magnificent pale blue bergère crinoline and I was in an embroidered, bucket-sleeved frock-coat and wig similar to the portrait of my ancestor, Lord Haversham, hanging on the dining room wall. Masks could be taken off at midnight, but till then, we were *incognito* and could behave as badly as we liked.

It was summer, the house was floodlit and in the garden was a tented pavilion serving food and drink. But the main banquet was in the dining room, with dancing in the drawing room.

On arrival, each guest was invited to be photographed on the stairs. Only one couple declined. Douglas and Sarah Hogg were careful not to create a photographic hostage for journalists.

We got a letter from one of our guests:

Dearest Jane,

What a sensational party! You and Richard gave us a wonderful evening in your beautiful house and your guests rewarded you with their spectacular costume dress. Thank you both for stimulating us into all making the effort for something entirely different. It did everyone a power of good, although a few grumbles must have echoed round the countryside at seven o'clockish as staid men grappled with hose and wigs! But once there it was a complete delight, and the mask idea was brilliant. The 'wenches' worked so hard, as did the serving-men, and the band were an excellent, if strange, combination of Georgian costume, rocking and rolling away. The house is looking wonderful – you are doing an amazing job. (Sallie Wood)

We had proved that the house was ideal for parties and in subsequent years we had concerts, opera, antiques roadshow, a reception for neurologists, garden parties, and the village fetes. But best of all was Alice and Richard's wedding in 1991.

By 1991 the drawing room was fully restored. It measures 36ft. × 24ft. and together with the dining room, the hall and the

Alice and Richard's wedding. April 1991

library, we were able to accommodate 250 people at Alice's wedding reception. The drawing room ceiling is probably the most outstanding feature of the house interior with near life-size plaster figures in 9 inch relief at all the four sides. And in the centre is a huge Adamesque rose from which the chandelier hangs. The walls were painted in the original apricot colour. When the house was built from 1784 to 1787 no curtains were hung, and instead they relied on shutters. On our travels to China after a medical meeting in 1987, Jane found some beautiful peacock blue silk which was very cheap. We struggled back to England with four bolts of silk as hand luggage; and in due course, Jane made the six curtains for the drawing room, which measured nearly 13 feet high.

For the wedding service only a hundred could be fitted into St James's Church at the bottom of the garden. After the service a marching band led the bride and groom and their guests through the garden to the house. It was April and all the daffodils were out. I was intensely proud of my lovely daughter and I was delighted that she had found Richard Cunningham such a charming, able and intelligent young man.

Both of our children seemed happy and successful. They were everything that Jane and I could have wished for.

Only one dark cloud began to develop at that time. It was a dispute with our neighbour Mrs Sherwin, and a man friend, Mr Widdowson. And the issue was the placing of the boundary between our properties to the east of the Hall.

Mrs Sherwin had been friendly with Ernest Ottewell, and when he bought the Papplewick Hall estate she persuaded him to sell her the link block with the Hall, which she named Chetwynd House. The boundary ran in a straight line at a right angle to the house. One day we woke to find that a fence on the boundary had been moved in Mrs Sherwin's favour to take in some ten feet of land. All our attempts at discussion were rudely rebuffed. After several such attempts, we decided to instruct a surveyor who duly placed marker posts where the true boundary ran.

A few days later, I was at work, but Jane looked out to see Mr Widdowson and two men preparing to remove the surveyor's marker posts. She went out and in the argument that ensued she put her hand on the top of the post to prevent its removal. One of the men then brought an iron bar down on her hand. Jane retired seriously hurt and in tears. She had a nasty soft tissue injury.

At this stage, we realised that we would have to take legal action, but the process dragged on for three years. All our attempts at compromise were rejected with their argument that Ottewell had decided the boundary and he would give evidence in Court for them – whatever the plans, Land Register or survey might say.

The case was drawn up, statements were given, Expert Witness reports were received and Counsel was briefed. The first day in Court was set for a Monday.

On the Sunday before the Court hearing the telephone rang. A voice that I did not recognize asked to speak to Mrs Godwin-Austen. He then explained: 'I was the man with Mr Widdowson who hit your hand and it has been troubling me ever since.'

We had been advised not to make much of the hand injury which had healed well; but to concentrate on the boundary issues. But the strange voice on the telephone continued: 'I know you go to Court tomorrow. I know you are right and because I'm sorry for what I did, I would like to come to Court to give evidence for you.'

Jane asked him to be at Court an hour before the case was due to start. With difficulty, we contacted our barrister, who interviewed our new witness at 9.00 a.m. And he was the first witness to take the oath. The Judge allowed him to give his address in writing because the witness explained that there might be violence against him if Mr Widdowson knew where he lived.

The evidence of this witness lasted twenty minutes. It was utterly convincing and devastating to our opponents. Their side requested an adjournment and when the Court reassembled they conceded defeat, and agreed to pay all costs. The boundary was restored to its true position and our opponents had a bill for more than £36,000.

The hero of this triumph was our unexpected witness. Christmas was approaching and Jane wanted to give him a present, but he still would not give us his name or address. He said: 'I won't come to your house because Sherwin or Widdowson might see me.'

Finally, it was decided that a turkey would be handed over the wall at the bottom of the garden. And so it was; every year before Christmas until Jane died, Mr X. received his Christmas present of a large turkey in the lane to the church at the bottom of our garden.

There was one further significant event that concerned Ernest Ottewell. A parcel of land big enough to build a house on and adjacent to our garden had been retained by Ottewell. Through my agents, I tried to buy back this land but I was surprised to be told, in all seriousness, that Ottewell would only accept payment in gold Rand and paid into a numbered bank account in Switzerland. I was therefore not surprised when I heard that the Serious Fraud Office were investigating Ernest Ottewell. In due course he was taken to Court but pleaded, on the basis of a medical report, that he was developing Alzheimer's disease and couldn't remember.

He then fled to Ireland where he was reported to be living in a house belonging to Mr Haughey, ex-president of Ireland, who was a long-standing friend and with whom he had much in common.

When we were visiting Jonathan at St Andrews University, we had seen a notice advertising

WHY NOT OWN A BENTLEY FOR LESS THAN THE PRICE OF A SECOND-HAND MINI?

I could not resist a bargain, and offered the vendor the full price, on condition that he delivered the car to my front door in Nottingham. I expected the vehicle to be unable to manage the 500 mile journey. Thus I was somewhat surprised to find the Bentley delivered about three weeks later. It was a beautiful motor car, built in 1952 but in a sorry state. I found a patient, Mr Hustwayte, living in Lincolnshire who was expert at motor car restoration. My car therefore went into his workshop and remained there for some six or seven years! It was slowly restored to its former greatness – at the same time as we were restoring Papplewick Hall. In 1995, with the start of my High Sheriff year, both these projects came to fruition. The Hall was largely restored, and in particular the interior was very fine. My car had been repainted maroon and black and seemed a suitable form of transport for a Sheriff to attend the functions. It was therefore with some confidence that I embarked on the most enjoyable year, acting as High Sheriff for the county of Nottingham and serving Her Majesty's Judges on the Oxford and Midlands Circuit.

CHAPTER 11

The High Sheriff: a great honour

UNLESS ONE IS PERSONALLY CONNECTED to the Shrievalty most people are hardly aware of the existence or function of the High Sheriffs. And even when one has had the experience of the year in office it is difficult to explain the role of the High Sheriff or to justify it. The High Sheriffs of England are a remnant of history associated with ceremonial and uniform. It is a good example of an Office of State whose original purpose has almost entirely disappeared. Like the College of Arms, the Shrievalty must be accepted as an anachronism, but also as something that needs to be preserved to remind us of our history and of the importance of the judiciary and of our legal system. The office of the High Sheriff is appointed by the Crown and is unpaid. Among comparable appointments, High Sheriffs are less important than the magistracy and older than the Lord Lieutenancy. High Sheriffs are nominated for each county in England and Wales for one year. But they are strictly unnecessary in their primary function to support the judges on the High Court bench during their visits to the County Court. They have a minor place to bring ceremonial to the county for events ranging between the Queen's official birthday and Remembrance Day at one extreme, to opening fetes and giving prizes for civic distinction at the other. Efforts have been made to increase contemporary relevance but it is largely true that the Shrievalty remains a harmless example of what the British do well – show respect for ancient traditions. Above all it costs the State nothing and the office has no political power, nor any legal influence.

I was nominated to serve the twelve months starting on the first Wednesday after Easter 1994. The nomination had been approved by the Queen three years before. Because I survived the three years and had not been brought before the Courts for any offence during this time I was deemed to be suitable to take up office.

I had also had to make careful arrangements to cover my medical work and in this I was fortunate to have the support of my neurologist colleagues David Jefferson and Alan Whiteley. I had to fit my outpatients clinics and ward rounds into the schedule of the High

Sheriff which meant working a three session day rather than a two session one.

In the previous November, I had attended with Jane at the Royal Courts of Justice in the Strand to receive the final official nomination from the Lord Chancellor and the Lord Chief Justice. The names were read out county by county and included Antony Butterwick for the county of Greater London, who was married to my friend of thirty-five years ago – Joanna Vanderfelt, whom I had not seen since my break-up with Sally Toller.

The appointment ceremony was held in the magnificent Georgian Newark Town Hall, where I took over from Juliet Mortensen, and was sworn in by Marcia Abel Smith JP. It was the first time that I had appeared in the official uniform of the High Sheriff – Court dress circa 1760 – black velvet tailcoat and breeches, black tights, buckled shoes and Nottingham lace jabot and cuffs, gloves, bicorne hat and Court-sword. I had been advised to carry a tin of black boot polish in case there was the need to camouflage a ladder in the tights! The uniform looks elegant and impressive when you are standing up with the sword in its scabbard hanging clear of the tail-coat, but it is not possible to sit down without removing the sword and scabbard from its harness. When standing up after a church service or at the rising of the Court there was a somewhat unseemly struggle as I tried in gloves to thread my sword into the harness under my coat.

Where there were children watching a ceremonial procession, they usually wanted a demonstration that the sword was real and not just a plastic pantomime sword. I had to be careful not to draw the sword in public. There was also the need to be careful when I was in uniform and was served soup at a meal. Here it was difficult to avoid the lace cuffs falling into the minestrone. There was then the task of wringing-out the soup into a napkin and tucking the cuffs away. Sometimes I felt that dignity was a hair's breadth from descending into farce.

On one occasion I was sitting on a separate chair at the front of the church in a service of commemoration. The Scouts and Guides had processed and stood in a row immediately in front of me. We rose and standing to attention sang the National Anthem. The group leader in front of me was holding a large banner on a long flagpole. During the National Anthem the banner was slowly lowered in salute, but no attention was paid to the end of the flagpole nearest to me. This started perhaps two feet in front of me but as it was lowered the pole moved between my ankles and gradually ascended between my knees threatening to cause not just embarrassment but a possible injury. Fortunately, the group leader was small. The banner salute was completed with the flagpole between the thighs of my velvet breeches, and I was relieved to know that we would be singing only one verse of the National Anthem.

Nottingham is a major High Court on the Oxford and Midlands circuit. The presiding High Court judges try mostly criminal cases that are often beyond anything I had imagined. The depths to which human beings can descend in evil, amoral, violent and perverted behaviour is astonishing. Increasingly, I grew to respect the extraordinary professionalism of the police and the intellectual power and humanity of the judges.

Nearly all the judges were younger than I. Before their appointment to the High Court many had, as barristers, practised in an area of the law where they never saw a criminal case. The High Sheriff has the great privilege of seeing the workings of the mind of a judge while he deliberates upon a difficult case.

For example:

– was the accused sane at the time of the murder? His subsequent insanity is real but stands in the way of him attending court to hear the evidence against him; or

– the female party to outrageous perverted sexual activity dies from internal injuries. The law says, 'You may not consent to physical assault.' But it is also the law that, 'A sexual act between consenting adults in private' is legal.

The judge commented to me outside the Court that the Crown Prosecution Service should never have brought this case. Instead they should have explained to the relatives of the deceased that (a) they cannot get a conviction, and (b) they don't want the matter to be discussed in public.

Before I was High Sheriff I had little appreciation of the dangers and difficulties that the police had in assembling evidence to achieve a conviction by a jury. In Nottingham much of the most violent crime appeared to stem from gang warfare. But was witnesses' evidence to be trusted? Or was it merely an attempt to put in prison the gang who were your opponents?

Perhaps the saddest cases that came to Court were the crimes of passion. I will never forget the cry of the man who was found guilty of murdering his alcoholic wife. 'I still loved her when she was sober!'

There was also the lonely bank official, who suffered blackmail and extortion after he had been enticed into a homosexual relationship with an eighteen-year-old. 'I thought he loved me.'

One of the duties of a High Sheriff is to award an accolade to members of the public who have assisted the police at great risk to themselves. An individual on my list for such an accolade was Mr Elliott, who while travelling as a passenger in his brother's car noticed two men in an adjacent car holding down a young woman, who had blood on her face. Mr Elliott jumped out of his car, and challenged the driver, who then started to drive off. Mr Elliott immediately climbed onto the roof of the car and shouted to his brother to telephone the police. The driver attempted to throw him off the roof by driving at speed, but Mr Elliott clung onto the roof rack. When they stopped in traffic, Mr Elliott reached with his right hand through the driver's window and removed the keys from the ignition. He then ran to a nearby house and again telephoned the police, who made an arrest.

Outside the court, it is the job of the High Sheriff to introduce the judges to suitable individuals living in the county and to arrange social entertainment. Jane and I gave seventeen dinner parties for twenty-four High Court judges and their spouses. These were most agreeable occasions and many lasting friendships were made. There were occasional crises – cream spilt down the dinner jacket of an eminent judge; or the evening when the dog ate all the first course laid out in the places of the dinner party for fourteen.

I had a spat with a former High Sheriff who complained in a letter to a judge that this judge and his colleagues were outstaying their welcome on these occasions by not leaving until after 11:15 p.m. A copy of the letter was sent to me. I was very angry and replied to say that I profoundly disagreed with his eccentric opinion and felt ashamed of the insult. However my suggestion that a letter of apology was in order was not taken up and I had to apologise on his behalf.

The convention to return hospitality received was followed, especially by the judges who entertained generously in the Lodgings, entirely at their own expense. Usually two judges and their wives would entertain a dinner party of ten. We were served by Mr Lane the butler, and the meal was prepared by Mrs Lane. On average judges stayed for four to six weeks. During this time, they would have a weekly semi-official lunch for the barristers who were appearing in the case before them; and a weekly dinner party. They had to arrive with wine sufficient to provide for this entertaining and at least one judge brought his own silver. I know this because the tale was told how the tray of silver slithered out of the back of his car leaving spoons and forks scattered over the motorway on his journey to Nottingham. His Honour was seen retrieving as much as he could from the hard shoulder.

Guests at our dinner parties also generously returned hospitality. Usually these were delightful friendly occasions – but some were agonising. I remember being invited to a dinner with an elderly county couple. He was unexpectedly ill, and his wife was not used to coping without him. They had also invited a Chinese couple, who scarcely spoke all evening. We struggled through dinner and when the pudding was served, her ladyship approached with a half bottle of Muscat. As she poured a little into my thimble-sized glass, she exclaimed, 'Whoops – you are only meant to have a mouthful of this nectar!'

The highlight of the High Sheriff's year in Nottinghamshire is a service to mark the Queen's Official Birthday held in Southwell Minster, and usually followed by a large lunch party for those attending the service in an official capacity. The arrangements were largely the responsibility of the Under Sheriff, Richard Bullock, who held the invitation list. The organisation by the Under Sheriff was always impeccable, but however important the occasion, Richard Bullock always had the appearance of complete confidence. He never fussed and always kept his voice down.

His List of Invitees to the Minster included:

The Lord Lieutenant and his deputies.
The Judges.
The Civics – that is the Lord Mayors and the Mayors of the County, Cities and towns of Nottinghamshire.
The Inspector of Police, and his deputy.
The Head of the Fire Service and the Probation Service.
The Coroner.
Past High Sheriffs and those in nomination.
All their partners . . . 'and a great many more of a lesser degree' – adding up to about six hundred.

Jane's trumpet banners. High Sheriff 1994

In the week before the great day, final arrangements were made with the Provost, David Leaning and with the Head Verger, John Meredith. The timing and order of the processions was finalised; the placing of the trumpeters for the fanfare, and displaying the banners with my Coat of Arms (sewn by Jane); and the placing of the band, who were to play the voluntaries before and after the service.

A video was to be taken to record the service and we had to decide on the placement of video cameras, including one on the ledge beneath the West window. This ledge is two feet wide and about thirty-five feet above the stone floor of the nave with no parapet or hand rail. The cameraman seemed entirely confident about this arrangement. However, as we were concluding our discussions, he turned to me and said, 'We have met before. I was one of your patients. I saw you for epileptic fits!'

To which I nervously replied, 'I hope my treatment was successful.'

'Oh yes . . . I won't have a fit and fall . . . there have been none for two years.'

'Be sure to take the tablets!'

Jane and I drove to Southwell for the service with my family flag flying on the Bentley. Sir Andrew Buchanan, Lord-Lieutenant, and I processed together into the Minster with a splendid eight part fanfare of trumpets. After the service with the band playing Henry VIII's march, there was the usual gathering on the grass of the Close. There were many of my patients, including Hustwayte (who had restored the Bentley), doctors and secretaries from the hospitals and so many friends and neighbours. With Jane's help, I was able to bring most names to mind.

And then back to the Hall where the Newstead Miners Welfare Band, in their scarlet tunics, were playing in the sunshine. Lunch for eighty-four was served inside the house. But we had pudding with 'demi-sec' (sweet) champagne on the lawn.

I had invited the High Sheriff of Derbyshire, Gillian Hutchinson, to my service and in due course I attended her service in Derby Cathedral. Also attending was Michael Frampton, High Sheriff of South Yorkshire. We were seated together with Mrs Frampton on my left. Before the service, she said, 'He always goes to sleep on these occasions so dig him in the ribs to wake him up.'

Sure enough, through lessons and sermon, the High Sheriff slumbered, only snorting into temporary wakefulness when I surreptitiously nudged him.

One of the many privileges of being High Sheriff is the opportunity to visit industries, and the provision of services, in the county. I gave my under sheriff a list and Richard Bullock wrote the necessary requests. In this way, I had a chance to experience a morning with the police 'speed cop' on the motorway, and a visit to the police drug squad; the Galleries of Justice exhibition; the British Horological Institute; Trent Bridge cricket ground; and the main Sorting Office for the Postal Services. But the most interesting visits were to Ratcliffe-on-Soar Power Station; and down a coal mine at Thoresby pit.

The power station, I was told, is capable of supplying 15 per cent of all the electricity needs of the whole country. We were taken to a platform at the top of the furnace 175 feet above the ground, where powdered coal is blown into the furnaces burning as it falls and

heating steam to drive the turbines to a temperature of 568°C. They
burn 800 tonnes of coal every hour, and since the miners' strike, they
have kept a stockpile of 1.5 million tonnes of coal. It was altogether
an awesome experience, but scarcely less impressive than the colliery.

We arrived at Thoresby pit at 8 a.m. to be welcomed by the Mayor
of Mansfield. His wife took Jane off to change, and with the mayor,
I was taken to strip naked and change every article of clothing; watch
and ring were removed and we dressed in black pants and T-shirt,
orange overall, socks, 'bovver-boots', helmet, lamp, gloves and shin
pads. We then bent double to enter the cage, and dropped 2,000 feet
at 40 fps to the tunnel of the 'deep soft' seam. We then travelled on
a 'six-man paddy' train car through the darkness. We were taken two
miles underground to the 'drift'. And finally a one-mile walk to the
coalface. It was very hot with a forced draught at 80 to 90°F. We
were all sweating, with coal dust sticking to our faces and dribbling
down our necks.

The machinery was massive and the noise prevented any communication. The seam was six feet high and cut by two circular
cutters which tore the coal off the face at the rate of 32 tonnes per
minute. It fell onto a wide conveyor belt. The ceiling from where
the coal had been cut was supported by massive hydraulic beams,
which, after each cut along a 100-yard face, 'walked' forward six feet
allowing the roof to collapse behind us.

To get out we walked, stooped down, under five foot rings which
were buckling under the weight of the rock above us; and finally we
crawled through an exit gate to our 'paddy' for the return journey.

The sight of the Mayor of Mansfield, a large man, stripped naked,
and showering is one I shall always treasure in my memory. We
changed and the mine-manager, Mr Betts gave us an excellent cold
lunch. I had then to go on to see my patients at the hospital and
conduct a ward round as usual.

On the scale of experience, if a coal mine is at one extreme, the
opposite extreme, must be a Garden Party at Buckingham Palace.

We parked the Bentley with its 'X' windscreen sticker in the Mall
and walked through the forecourt gates into the inner courtyard: then
up the steps into the entrance hall. A gallery led to the bay room
opening onto a terrace and finally into the garden. It was very hot in
the bright sunshine, and we needed the iced coffee and ice creams
that were proffered. The Queen and the Prince of Wales worked

hard, moving slowly between the lines of 'Pikemen' of the Yeoman
of the Guard; and all the while, hovering in morning coat and top
hat, gentlemen-in-waiting wore dignified smiles as they provided the
Queen's real bodyguard while presenting guests to her.

We drove home in the cool evening relishing the experience and
arrived there at 1.00 a.m. On the journey Jane and I talked of events
unconnected with the Shrievalty. Two important things occupied
our minds. Alice's father-in-law was engaged to be married to Zoe,
having lost his wife shortly after his eightieth birthday. We were so
happy to know that he was going to put his life together again after
this tragedy. And our Jonathan at the rather younger age of
twenty-nine seemed also to be moving towards marriage to the
lovely Mary Cavender whom we had recently met. They were
obviously so happy and seemed so suited to each other.

Before finishing my year as High Sheriff I arranged a dinner for
the High Sheriffs in the Grand Jury Room of the Shire Hall, which
was the Old Court House for the City of Nottingham. The dinner
had been prepared with the greatest difficulty, because there were no
kitchen facilities. The electrics fused under the strain and an
electrician had to be summoned. But in the end Heather Wilkinson
triumphed and presented forty-six High Sheriffs and their spouses
with an excellent meal.

Looking back on my year, I thought about all the privileges that I
had enjoyed: meeting with Royalty and High Court judges; meeting
with the County – the 'Civics' – Mayors, Officers and Chairmen;
and learning much about the activities of the Courts, the Police and
other services. I could never have done it without the support and
sheer hard work of my dear Jane, who at all times looked beautiful
and distinguished. And she showed by her manner how much she
enjoyed it all. Terrible to know now that she had barely a year to
live.

PART 2

The New Life

CHAPTER 12

The ABN, WFN and retirement

BETTER WRITERS THAN I have given descriptions of the experience of bereavement and grief. It is beyond my skills to do justice to the subject. Suffice to say that the feeling is inescapable and all encompassing. The sense of loss is palpable day and night and invades every activity and thought. Nothing can ease the suffering – neither the company of friends or family, nor work, alcohol or recreation.

I received over 500 letters of condolence. Many were from friends who had suffered a similar experience. All were thoughtful, kind and often inspiring. And two letters gave advice which I found truly helpful.

The first was from a friend who had been suddenly widowed after eight years of marriage leaving her with two children to bring up.

'You will never get over your loss,' she said. 'People will tell you that time heals – it doesn't. The experience will leave you with a raw stump which you will carry for the rest of your life. But life does go on and happy new experiences accumulate to make it worth living.'

Another wrote: 'There are two rules that I tried to follow – Never allow yourself to say "Why me?" and never think the thought "If only . . ."'

I resolved to look forward and, as best I could, to start to build a new life. Shortly after Jane died I had been elected President of the Association of British Neurologists (ABN). When my injuries had healed I returned to work with the added responsibility associated with the ABN. There were committees to chair, meetings to organise and social events to host where to have Jane with me would have been wonderful. But never think 'if only . . .'

My children were an enormous support. They felt the loss of their mother terribly and the shared grief brought us even closer. Alice had spoken to Jane three days before the accident to tell her that she was pregnant with her second child. It was a comfort to know that Jane had enjoyed this happy news. Jonathan was married to Mary six months before Jane died and it was good that Mary had known Jane for almost a year. There were also the wedding photographs with everyone looking so happy.

President, Association of British Neurologists

As the weeks passed my friends started inviting me to dinner and introducing me to single friends they knew. It was strange to be single again myself and to be the object of interest for that reason. James Kirkman from Charterhouse-days took me out to lunch and suggested that I spend a week in Mexico in the new house they were building. Clare and James expected it to be finished by the end of January the next year and I accepted the invitation readily.

But the immediate concern was to arrange a holiday with my family and grandson, Rory. We decided that one week fishing in Scotland at a time to encompass my birthday would be suitable. The fishing was a great success but I caused embarrassment at my birthday party.

The children had organised a bagpiper for the celebration. When I opened Alice's present it was an amaryllis bulb pictured with a beautiful orange-pink flower; but the name 'Lady Jane' finished me, and I had to flee the room, completely overcome.

There were many practical domestic problems through being single, with two dogs in a large house and working full-time. I engaged a housekeeper who prepared an evening meal for me, lit the fire and walked the dogs. Walter Glew, our tenant aged eighty-one, was occupying the flat over the garage and had been very helpful walking the dogs. He abruptly gave notice 'because I can't bear the stress of losing Jane'. I therefore had to arrange a rota of individuals to take the dogs out in the daytime while I was at work and this was probably the cause of the next crisis.

Jennie was eight years old, and a beautiful springer spaniel whom I had trained to work as a gun dog. She was getting past her prime but her daughter was then four and was proving also to be an excellent gun dog. Gradually through the summer the dogs' attitude to each other changed. They became jealous of small favours and would occasionally growl at each other. The situation steadily deteriorated and then they started to fight. I had to first feed them separately, then walk them separately and finally they had to sleep separately to prevent them going at each other. The fights drew blood. I could see that one of them would actually kill the other if I didn't do something. I rang the Secretary of the English Springer Spaniel Association for advice, hoping that medication or even psychotherapy might provide the answer. But the news was bad.

'You will have to get rid of one of them, and nobody will take the older dog — it will have to be Pippa of Papplewick who goes.'

Sadly I placed the advertisement, found someone who would take her and arranged a rendezvous at a motorway service area for the hand-over.

I spent a miserable week leading up to the Sunday appointed for Pippa's departure. On the Saturday I was sitting with Pippa when the telephone rang. It was my housekeeper whom I seldom saw because by the time I got home during the week she had prepared my supper and left.

'I hear that you are getting rid of one of the dogs.'

She knew the problem, but I then told her the advice I had been given.

'Would you let me have her?' she said.

'But would you take Jennie even though she is eight years old?'

'Of course, that would be better for us — she is less bumptious.'

So I cancelled the arrangement for the following day; and Jennie went to a good home where she continued to go out shooting. Six

years later she died and was buried in a small copse close to the Hall
where her daughter eventually joined her. Those two dogs spanned
twenty years of shooting in Nottinghamshire and walking in the
woods of Papplewick Hall. The exercise kept us all fit and they both
were delightful companions.

From the time I had been High Sheriff I had been enrolled in the
'Shrievalty Association' along with all the other past and current High
Sheriffs. Once a year the Association held a meeting where the
accounts were approved and there was a social gathering and lunch.
And at the meeting that year I was surprised to see a face that I
vaguely recognised from long ago. I racked my brains and then, of
course, it was Joanna Vanderfelt whom I had not seen since 1958 (see
Chapter 4). I reminded her about the remote history and she went
on to explain that she had married Anthony Butterwick who had
been High Sheriff of Greater London. Once these pieces of
information had been exchanged, I asked Joanna whether she kept in
touch with Sally Toller whom I had not heard of since 1957. Yes,
she had met her about eight years ago when Joanna was in America,
but she did not know her address or married name. She understood
that Sally was not happy and thought that she would be interested to
hear from me. However, there was not enough information to make
that possible and the subject was dropped. But after lunch Joanna
sought me out again.

'I have been thinking how you could get hold of Sally's address,'
she said. 'I have the address of her cousin, JohSeb Peake at home —
I'll phone you with it tonight.'

I had met JohSeb at the 4th of June at Eton in 1956 and in due
course I wrote reminding him of this acquaintanceship and asking after
his cousin, Sally, who had introduced us forty years ago. The following
evening the telephone rang and it was JohSeb with all the humour and
enthusiasm that I remembered from long ago. He was *sure* Sally would
like to hear from me. He implied that things had not gone well for her
but I realised that I could not question him on this. He gave me the
address and married name and he insisted that I must write . . .

It took me several hours to compose a short letter.[9] I thought how
much she would have changed. She was probably now overweight,
elderly, self-absorbed and certainly nothing like the laughing girl that
I remembered. But she was alive and it would be fun to reminisce in
uncompromising circumstances. I suggested meeting for lunch if she

was ever on this side of the Atlantic. Nothing happened for three weeks and I had largely given up hope. Then there was a letter to say that she had just returned from a holiday but was coming to England in about six weeks and would love to meet for lunch. And so it was arranged.

She was staying in a friend's flat in London and I picked her up in my car and drove to the lunch date. I was extremely nervous of putting myself into a situation I would regret. But I was immediately reassured to note two things. The first was that Sally was at least as nervous as I was, and the second was that she had not changed. It was the same laughing, bubbly, beautiful girl that I remembered. The lunch lasted a long time and by the end of it I had heard her description of the forty years that had passed, and I was planning when we could meet again. I thought that I detected that Sally felt likewise.

Her visit to England was scheduled to last six weeks and aimed to progress the book that she was writing on the *Portraits of Queen Victoria*. It was my fault that less progress was made than she hoped. We saw a lot of each other – it was as if the relationship was developing from where it had left off forty years earlier. However, her first visit to Papplewick did not go as planned.

I had suggested a weekend and I collected Sally from the station on a bitterly cold night on my way home from work. I had asked my housekeeper – who from that time was nicknamed 'Mrs Danvers' – to prepare us a meal and to light the fire as usual. When we reached Papplewick Hall I sensed something was wrong. Mrs Danvers had left an enormous dish of unappetising spaghetti bolognaise and the fire was burning. But it was burning much too fast. Mrs Danvers had wanted the house to be warm and welcoming. She had piled the wood-burning stove with logs, opened all the ventilation and gone home. I excused myself and went out on the lawn. The chimney pot looked like an erupting volcano with sparks and flames roaring. The Fire Brigade arrived about 9.00 p.m. and worked all night, finally leaving at about 6.00 a.m.

There was some sixty feet of burning chimney, which was divided into six sections. The walls were so hot you couldn't bear to touch them. With a stirrup pump each section was extinguished in turn and steel buckets of hot wet soot were carried downstairs and emptied into my steel wheelbarrow. In the dark I was the only one who knew where to empty it. Sally meanwhile was assumed by the firemen to know the house and where to direct them to hoses, water taps and brooms. To save embarrassment at her plight she retired to her room and, I believe, slept quite well, no doubt dreaming of her 'return to Manderley'.[10]

When I had been working for Barney Alcock in Devon I learnt that his biannual Study Leave to attend the 'ABN Meetings' was sacrosanct. He always insisted on attending every meeting of the Association of British Neurologists. He explained that it kept him up-to-date, enabled him to discuss patients and practice with colleagues and to keep up with neurological politics. When I was later elected a Junior Member I followed his example and this continued when I acquired full Membership of the ABN, on appointment as Consultant. The meetings lasted two days; the Spring Meeting was held outside London and the Autumn Meeting always in London. Twenty short papers reporting research projects and lectures reviewing current practice completed the programme. During the breaks and in the evening old friendships were renewed and new friendships were made. One important function of these meetings was for the consultant staff to assess the young neurologists in training for future hospital appointments. It was the responsibility of the consultant to know the capabilities of junior career neurologists, and their suitability for specific appointments. His responsibility was also to determine the development and improvement of the neurological services provided by his department, including the introduction of new technology, which would be an important part of presentations at the ABN.

Perhaps the most important technical development in neurology in the last thirty years has been the invention and application of MRI scanning. The initial research into creating an image using magnetic resonance was conducted in the Physics Department in the University of Nottingham by Bill Moore. He had the genius to appreciate the possibility of imaging the magnetic resonance of hydrogen atoms using the imaging technique developed for CAT scanning by Sir Godfrey Hounsfield. Bill Moore first produced an MRI image of an onion; then one of his own wrist and because he had suffered no adverse effect, the first MRI image of the head – his own. At this stage he needed to involve the co-operation of clinical colleagues to consider the application of the technique in clinical practice. First Bryan Worthington (later Professor) became involved and I seized the opportunity to play a very small part by supporting the early investigations on patients. Some of our early results were presented to the ABN. But the first presentation of MRI scans of six patients with intracranial abnormalities was presented by me in Kyoto, Japan at the World Congress of Neurology in 1981. When I submitted the abstract to the organisers of that meeting (The World Federation of Neurology), the Programme Committee had no knowledge of Magnetic Resonance or its application. They were unable to understand the place or the significance of the work and while accepting my paper they suggested it should be given in a session on Neuropathology. This was wholly inappropriate. And the room available for this session seated only about forty people.

In due course I attended the session allocated. The presenter of the paper before mine failed to turn up and the Chairman suggested that I present my paper twenty minutes early. I was disappointed to have an audience of only about fifteen. After about ten minutes into my presentation the room began to fill up and by the time I came to the end some thirty people were standing, all the chairs were taken and they were unable to close the doors for people trying to push in. The first man to run the mile in under four minutes, Dr Roger Bannister, was one of the late-comers. I knew Roger well and had already told him in outline what I was presenting. When I sat down, Roger addressed the Chairman from the back of the room. 'We are all here to listen to the paper that has just finished. Would the Chairman please allow Dr Godwin-Austen to present his paper again.'

So I had to stand up and give the paper again. Before or since, I have never encountered the same paper being presented twice at the same meeting. But I have heard the same paper presented at several different meetings!

MRI was rapidly accepted as the premier method for imaging the central nervous system but sadly Bill Moore did not live to receive the recognition he so richly deserved. While on a lecture tour in the United States he suffered a heart attack and died. The only memorial that I know celebrating the man and his discoveries is a photograph of Bill Moore in the meeting room in the x-ray department at Queen's Medical Centre. I hope that it is still there.

My triumph in Kyoto made that a special meeting for me. It also introduced me to the World Federation of Neurology, a relationship which was to continue a long time.

In 1993 after the World Congress of Neurology in Vancouver, I was invited by the ABN to become British Delegate to the World Federation of Neurology (WFN). While the ABN is an association of individuals meeting together to promote best clinical practice in Neurology in the British Isles (Ireland included), the WFN is a Federation of National Neurological Societies represented by their Delegates with the mission to 'Promote Neurological Health World-wide'. The two organisations, therefore, have different purposes, the ABN to serve the individual neurologist; and the WFN to serve the development of Neurology globally. My appointment as Delegate to the WFN was for four years and therefore it overlapped with my two-year term as President of the Association of British Neurologists 1996–98. The year 1997 proved to be busy.

The Australian Association of Neurologists had as its President that year a very good friend of mine – Rick Burns. We had met when he was appointed my Assistant Registrar at the National Hospital for Neurology, Queen Square. Rick is a good example of all that is good in Australian manhood. He is athletic, extroverted, and enthusiastic. He is also intelligent, well trained, and a hard working neurologist. I was therefore very pleased when he sent an invitation, on behalf of the Australian Association to about thirty British neurologists, to attend their annual meeting in Sydney.

Sally and I flew out a week early and stayed with Rick and Renate in Adelaide. We had a good meeting in Sydney, the only disappoint-ment being that the Australian neurologists had to call off our challenge to a cricket match. The Poms were deprived of the pleasure of beating soundly the Aussie neurologists! Some hope!

A few months later we attended the World Congress of Neurology in Buenos Aires. For the avoidance of doubt (as the lawyers say) I was financing these trips out of my pocket so 1997 was an expensive year; but we loved Argentina. There was frost on the grass as we landed in Buenos Aires. We changed planes and flew to the Iguazu falls where we recovered from jet-lag. Again the meeting was excellent. A highlight was a talk on the effects of neurological illnesses in world leaders including Winston Churchill (multiple strokes) and Hitler (Parkinson's disease). There was a display of medical politics at its worst in the election for President when twelve candidates were proposed and harsh words were spoken. Under Lord Walton's masterly chairmanship no-one came to blows. The Latin-American

With Rick Burns, Pres. Aus. Assn. Neur., 1997 Adelaide, S. Australia

spirit must have affected our usually ultra-calm delegates. James Toole from Winston-Salem, North Carolina was elected President, and coincidently it was he who had given the talk on illness in world leaders.

The most important event in 1997 was yet to come. On 15 November Sally and I were married in St James's Church, Papplewick. During my speech at the reception there was a loud crash and some scuffling at the back of the room. I learned later that my cousin, Gilly (Gilbert) Marsh, had fainted but had quickly recovered. In his unnecessary letter of apology, Gilly explained that in falling he had hit his head on my harpsichord. But he hastened to emphasise that the harpsichord was undamaged and as for his head, the blow appeared to have relieved his deafness!

Retirement for me was a gradual process. First I gave up NHS work in South Lincolnshire where I had run a clinic in Boston for twenty-five years. Then I gave up my inpatient and outpatient work in Derby and changed to a part-time locum contract in Nottingham from the time of our wedding. I progressively reduced my private practice.

In the place of this tailing off of clinical work I took on honorary voluntary work of which the most important was the post of Secretary Treasurer General (STG) of the World Federation of

Sally 1998

Neurology. When I was being 'sounded out' whether I would accept nomination, the opportunities for travel were much emphasised. But I realised once in post that this was only one of the matters that needed reform.

In Buenos Aires the delegates had chosen London to be the venue for the next World Congress in 2001. This was probably the main reason I was chosen as 'STG'.

My predecessor, Frank Clifford Rose, had been STG for eight years. He had run the organisation using his Harley Street address and office with his wife giving enormous assistance especially when they both were attending meetings abroad. Important changes in communication had come about during the 'Clifford Rose Era' and I was able to establish inexpensive electronic communication for all the running of the WFN. This change was made possible because, thanks to the success of the previous administration, the WFN had resources sufficient to establish an office in London and to appoint Keith

Newton as administrator, and Susan Bilger as secretary. Through the new office I was able to run the WFN from Nottingham and to travel to London for important meetings. Gradually the emphasis of the organisation changed from what had been described by its critics as a 'travelling club' to an organisation with three main purposes.

We developed postgraduate education in neurology in developing countries – mainly in Central America and in Africa. We promoted collaboration with the WHO in the publication of material related to Public Health issues in Neurology. And we continued the very successful quadrennial World Congresses, promoting these meetings as the essential opportunity for neurologists worldwide to update their knowledge of best clinical practice.

But it was not all plain sailing. Individuals newly-elected to the position of Trustee started with the notion that the WFN was so rich they could have the pleasure of spending the money on their pet projects. I narrowly avoided large sums being given away to charity appeals that were not even neurological – such as the Honduras Hurricane Appeal. The biggest bombshell hit suddenly and unexpectedly when Keith Newton telephoned to tell me that my elected successor Julien Bogousslavsky was in prison on a charge of embezzlement. The first reaction was horror at the predicament of a friend and a colleague whose work I admired. But it became clear that the WFN must be protected from any possible wrongdoing even though the case would probably not come to trial for at least twelve months. Julien's resignation had to be obtained, The Charity Commission had to be informed and a successor to replace Julien had to be identified. Once again, Keith Newton found the solution to the replacement problem. He had kept the actual voting papers from the election. We could argue that if the information about the criminal charges laid had been available to the delegates, Julien's name would have been ineligible for the ballot. The votes were therefore re-counted using the second choice on all voting papers that had been cast for Julien; and Ra'ad Shakir was declared Secretary-Treasurer General elect.

In retrospect, working voluntarily for the WFN taught some useful management and administrative skills. In the medical profession such skills are not rated very high. But the experience left me with a greater understanding of how difficult it is for a manager without a medical background to judge priorities in the provision of medical services. Working for the WFN to improve neurological services in developing countries, the priorities are clear. First the training of young doctors in the ethics and medical skills needed, and then the provision of the appropriate facilities to exercise those skills and to maintain them ('continuing medical education'). The NHS is declining because instead of making the needs of the individual patient drive the priorities of the service, it is driven by financial incentives rather than professional ones. The health outcome for the patient is what matters, not minor statistics that are easy to measure and have little effect on the quality of the result of treatment, such as waiting times, targets and 'consultant episodes'. But I digress.

The chief source of income for the WFN came from the profits of the World Congresses and these profits resulted essentially from two things. Firstly, from the reputation that we had earned for organising meetings which attracted substantial numbers of neurologists; and secondly, from the support of the pharmaceutical industry. The meeting in London in 2001 built on the success of Buenos Aires and laid some of the foundations for the huge success in Sydney, Australia in 2005. But if one can be complacent in retrospect, it is salutary to recall how nearly our successes were turned to failure.

In Buenos Aires three months after the World Congress there was collapse of the Argentine currency and the country went into political and financial crisis. If these events had been a few months earlier the Congress would undoubtedly have failed.

In London the date of the Congress was originally scheduled for late September or early October. It was rescheduled to June, because of the unavailability of an appropriate venue. On 11 September 2001 the '9/11' events would have prevented the Congress in London if it had remained scheduled for the autumn.

And in Sydney, Australia, the Congress was in its first week when the police authorities acknowledged the investigation of terrorist activities in Sydney and made arrests. If this announcement had been made a month earlier many would have cancelled their attendance.

So we were lucky and the recognition of the Federation's vulnerability has led to a cautious 'Reserves Policy' being established. And as it was, Sally and I had a wonderful time in Sydney, meeting again the friends who had entertained us so generously in 1997; and making new friends from around the world. We spent a few days after the meeting recovering in Tasmania and then flew to Vietnam to board a vessel on the Mekong which sailed to Angkor Wat.

CHAPTER 13

San Miguel de Allende

THE ATTENTIVE READER OF THIS memoir may wonder what the outcome was of the invitation from James and Clare Kirkman for me to stay at their new home in San Miguel de Allende, Mexico. He or she will also recall that James Kirkman had shared the flat in Oakfield Street in 1957 when I had been going out with Sally. When I met Sally again some weeks before I was due to stay in Mexico I reminded James of her and he immediately suggested that it would be nice if she also came to Mexico. She readily accepted and in February 1997 we had our first encounter with colonial Mexico.

San Miguel de Allende is a town with a long, complex and distinguished history. Ignatio Allende was one of the leaders of the Revolution in 1812 and Aldama (whose name is commemorated in the street where the Kirkman's house was situated) was a foremost General in the revolutionary forces. The town was made wealthy by the discovery of gold and silver in the mountains nearby and it developed with the building of magnificent palaces, churches and

San Miguel de Allende, Mexico

town houses in the sixteenth century. There were also more modest workmen's houses laid out in a jumble of cobbled streets surrounding the centre of town and it was one of these that had been bought by James and Clare and converted.

The house was just finished and we were their first guests. We had a wonderful week exploring the town, visiting silver mines and meeting the Kirkmans' friends. We fell in love with the house and with the place.

From her first marriage, Sally had three sons, all of whom had been brought up and educated in America. By the time we were married the older two sons – Jonathan and Andrew – were also married. With her move to England, Sally began to miss being able to see her children. She also found the English winter in Papplewick Hall was long and cold. When James and Clare Kirkman announced that they had restored a second house in San Miguel we decided to buy their first house and spend the cold months in England in the Mexican sunshine entertaining Sally's children and our friends from England and America.

On one occasion American friends had been with us and had a taxi booked to pick them up at about 6 a.m. on a Sunday morning to take them to the airport. Sally and I rose early in pyjamas and dressing gowns and helped them to carry their bags out to the taxi. We waved them goodbye and then turned to find that the front door had slammed shut and was firmly locked against us. The keys were inside; spare keys only at the letting agency – closed all day Sunday. It was 6 a.m., just before sunrise, quiet and beautiful but the scene was not fully appreciated in our predicament. We stood in the road in our pyjamas and discussed what we could do.

The house two doors down belonged to someone we had never met but we thought she might be English and might have a sense of humour. We rang the doorbell. By then it was 6.30 a.m. After a delay, when we did not want to ring again, the door opened a fraction and a young female English voice asked what we wanted. We explained and – 'Could we possibly climb on your roof, clamber over the roof next door and hence into our own property to let ourselves in?'

It sounded absurd but we clearly did not look like burglars. Lisa introduced herself as the niece of the owner – but she felt sure the owner wouldn't mind. And then she looked at the elderly couple in their pyjamas and she decided to offer to climb over the roofs for us. 'It would be safer.'

After this adventure Lisa and her aunt became good friends. Lisa married a delightful Mexican doctor and they still live in San Miguel de Allende.

The flights from England were long but comfortable, landing at Mexico City in the evening. On our second time to San Miguel we decided to travel the two hundred miles from Mexico City by road on a bus rather than in an expensive hired car. The first problem arose because we had set our watches wrongly on the instructions of the BA pilot. As a result we rose at 5.00 a.m. We did not understand why the hotel staff were surprised to see us at breakfast so early. We arrived at the bus station an hour early, still unaware of the correct time. In those days we had only minimal command of the Spanish language and I was in the habit of trying to identify anyone who might understand English and therefore be of potential assistance. At the bus stop was just such a person. A beautiful, well-dressed, middle-aged Mexican lady was holding an English magazine. I asked her if this was the right place to catch the bus to San Miguel and she replied in fluent English. She explained that we had a long wait because our watches were wrong.

When we arrived in San Miguel the bus station was almost deserted with no immediate sign of a taxi. The Mexican lady was close by and I saw a man coming towards us who looked like a taxi-driver. I turned to the lady and said, 'Is he a taxi man?'

To my astonishment the 'taxi man' said in perfect English, 'Yes, I am the taxi, where are you going?' and the lady said, 'No, it is my husband, he is joking but we would be happy to drive you.'

Yolande and Chato Perea became some of our firmest friends in San Miguel after this episode. He is an architect and we visited their ranch outside town and some of the houses he had built.

San Miguel de Allende was 'discovered' in the 1950s and became a favourite with artists from about that time. The town is extremely attractive with adobe terrace houses painted in yellows, terracotta, blue and magenta. The door surrounds and the mullions of windows are in carved stone which has a dark red hue. In the centre of town there is the main square where in the season almost daily festivities take place – marching bands, religious processions, school children parading or Aztecan dancers dressed in feather costumes and beating drums. The main square is surrounded on three sides by the grand stone houses of the sixteenth century families who established San Miguel. And on the fourth side are two churches – the 'Parochia' (or parish church) which is said to be designed by a builder creating a copy of postcard images of French cathedrals; and San Raphael – a less ebullient classical gothic building.

In recent times San Miguel has attracted visitors because it enjoys a comfortable climate all the year round. This also attracted us because in February/March the sun shines almost daily out of a deep blue sky and temperatures rise to the mid 70s. With solar panel heating we kept the swimming pool at 82°F.

About 10 per cent of the population in February are visitors from Canada, from the north-east of USA and from Texas. This has led to the development of entertainment facilities, such as theatre, concerts, and lectures. The social life can become hectic with lavish parties held in palatial houses. One of the most notable houses was that of a Texan widow who had converted a convent with cloisters, fountains and courtyards reminiscent of the Alhambra. The house was used for only a few weeks in the year when Martha came down with about twelve guests and gave a series of lavish lunch parties served by her staff of sixteen dressed in Mexican national costume.

When we had friends staying we liked to drive into the country to the silver mine at Pozos. The mine had been abandoned in 1967. The village was small and unspoilt and there was a hotel with three bedrooms. which also served lunch if you ordered it in advance by telephone. There was plenty to see and it was pleasant to walk among the ruined old mine buildings in the empty countryside.

The number of English house owners in San Miguel is quite small. We therefore noticed new English faces when they appeared. Piers de Laszlo was an example. As an artist he had decided to come to exhibit his work and to paint in San Miguel. We met at his exhibition. He was tall, untidy, with long unkempt hair, and charming. His grandfather was the celebrated Edwardian portraitist, and Piers is an extremely competent landscape and genre painter.

One day Piers had invited Sally and me to a party in the house he had just bought. It was small, and bohemian in its untidiness. We had a very good time at the party and at about midnight decided to walk home. As soon as we reached our door, I excused myself and rushed to the loo. But when I tried to come out, much relieved, I found the lock on the door was broken and I could not open it. I called to Sally but she also was unable to release me. The window opened onto the street and was barred so there was no escape. We thought about my predicament, conversing through the door. Should I spend the night sleeping in the bath – at least Sally would be able to pass food and drink, and bedding, between the bars on the window from the street. After a while (it was only about 1 a.m.) we decided that the party was probably still going, and Sally would ring Piers and ask him if he could bring friends from the party and tools to take the door off its hinges. He accepted the challenge only if we promised to 'make it fun' and allow the party to continue in our house once I was released. He was probably running a little low on alcohol. We readily agreed.

Shortly afterwards, a car drew up with a load of friends and heavy equipment to remove the door. I was soon released and it was two hours later that we all finally decided that it was time to end the party and to go to bed. I was considerably more comfortable than I would have been in the bath.

I had always wanted Sally to sit for her portrait. It seemed like a good opportunity to ask Piers whether he would consider painting her portrait while we were all in San Miguel. I broached the subject and after careful consideration, Piers agreed only on condition that no payment would be made unless both Piers and I were entirely satisfied with the result.

Sally sat for her portrait for four hours a day for ten days. And then, one morning Piers suddenly decided to show us the result. I was delighted. It was a good likeness and a handsome three-quarter length portrait. But Piers insisted that he did not want to continue, and was not satisfied. He picked up the portrait, left, and I have never seen it again. Such is the eccentricity of artists. But I am glad to say that this episode did not affect the friendship. 'One day' he has promised to do another portrait.

Epilogue

A T THE END, JANE WAS UNCONSCIOUS and did not suffer. And I was spared. I have been blessed with opportunities and much happiness, for which I am grateful. For Sally to come back into my life was nothing short of a miracle. And life together with Sally now is happier and more fulfilled than I could have ever dared to hope. I have the blessing of my children's happy and successful families, with six attractive grandchildren. Who could ask for more?

I cannot resist a final anecdote. I had driven to London and parked the car on the street. The day following was Saturday and I wrongly assumed that I need not feed any parking meter. When I came out I found not only a ticket but the car was clamped. I paid the £80.00 by credit card, and sat in the car waiting for the lorry to unclamp me. As I sat there a young man came down the pavement and stopped by

The grandchildren. From L – Harry GA, Coco C, George GA, self, Flora-Jane C,
Annie GA and Rory C (standing)

my car looking at the clamp. I wound down the window and he said, 'Just like me, I've also got a clamp.'

'I've paid mine and I am waiting to have it removed.'

'Trouble is I have no money on me. I left my credit card at home in Brighton.' After a pause he said, 'I say, would you be terribly kind and pay my clamp charge on your credit card? I'll send you a cheque tomorrow.'

After some further discussion, I took pity on him, thinking that he was unlikely to be in criminal collaboration with the clampers. He gave me his name, address, and telephone number in Brighton. I awaited his cheque with some trepidation.

There was nothing in the Tuesday post so I rang his number. His voice answered and he said, 'Don't worry, it's in the post.'

There seemed not much more that I could do, and I thought that he had made a fool of me. But I was wrong.

On Wednesday a cheque arrived with a very nice letter of thanks; and the cheque was not for £80, but for £100.

The Moral?

Most people that I have met in quite a long life have been kind, generous and trustworthy. Of course I am lucky, these memoirs prove it, but I believe that the enemies are mistrust, cynicism, and 'cool'. And happiness is seizing opportunities, commitment, gratitude and trust.

End notes

1   Rita Ghey, Letter (1923) in *A Rich Inheritance* (1992).
2   Corelli Barnett, *The Desert Generals* (1983).
3   H. Chochinov, 'Dignity and the Essence of Medicine', *BMJ* (2007) 335, 184.
4   Raymond Tallis, *Hippocratic Oaths* (2004).
5   Shelley Potter et al. 'Two week rule', *BMJ* (2007) 335, 288.
6   Con Coughlin, *Saddam, The Secret Life* (2002).
7   Newsweek 9 May 1977.
8   Con Coughlin *op. cit.*
9   Samuel Johnson, *I apologise for . . .* (c.1756).
10 Daphne du Maurier, *Rebecca* (1938).

Appendix

How to save the NHS without throwing further money at it

THE NHS HAS ALWAYS BEEN popular with its clients – the patients and their families. It used to be also the proud boast of the medical profession, who probably know, that the medical services in the UK were 'the best in the world'. You don't hear that claim now. Indeed, scarcely a day goes by without some NHS failure or crisis being reported in the press.

It used to be claimed that this country spent less per capita than other developed countries. It is now the proud boast of the Government that expenditure on the NHS is similar to Western European countries. But the medical services of the Western European countries are often perceived by the public to be better than ours. The patient here is aware of a service where there are more mistakes, no perceived improvement in accessibility, poorer outcome and where the old doctor-patient relationship no longer exists. The doctor is also full of complaints. His complaints centre around more abstract and amorphous matters: increased bureaucracy and form filling; management-driven and target-driven medical services, rather than care designed to fulfil the needs of the individual patient; and the loss of the power by the doctor to deliver improvements to the service. This has led to a service where such improvements can now be initiated only by management (especially if there are cost implications). So we are spending vastly more for a deteriorating health service. Why? Let us look first at standards and then at costs.

Standards of Practice in Medicine can ultimately only be set and maintained by the professions (medical and nursing). But the doctor is no longer asked for his advice by management and his warnings that 'it won't work because . . .' are ignored. How do doctors react to the patients' perception as suggested above, 'more mistakes and poorer outcome'? These are matters that are taken most seriously by the medical profession. They go to the heart of professional standards.

In most continental countries accreditation of doctors and assessment of standards of health care services are reviewed by committees of doctors, together with patients. And as Charles Shaw has pointed out: 'In England the Healthcare Commission (set up by Government) is abnormally resistant to sharing responsibility for safety and standards, with the providers and with the professions. Excellence, in motivation, learning and clinical systems . . . is the expertise of Professional Associations, educators and other providers (such as doctors) . . . with the Medical Royal Colleges the leader for standards of excellence.' (*JRSM* [2007] 100, 206–7)

The Department of Health, instead of consulting the established and experienced independent professional Colleges, has sought to marginalise their influence and replace them with quangos such as the Health Care Commission, the NICE Committee, and the Post-graduate Medical Education and Training Board. These bodies are the creatures of the Department of Health and are not independent. They are seen to be serving the needs of government policy, not the needs of the patient or of his agent – the doctor. And the costs are considerable – whereas formal consultation with the Colleges costs nothing.

One area of the National Health Service where the Department of Health must have full responsibility is in what used to be called Public Health Services. The political trend has been to confuse the boundary between public health issues on the one hand, and the treatment and care services for the individual patient on the other. For example, alcohol abuse is a serious public health issue and policy must be determined by Government. But the injuries sustained in a drunken brawl must receive the same medical care as injuries sustained otherwise. In order to do this the Health Services need to be shaped and modified by the providers, not managed centrally by the Government.

Public health services involve political decisions over the distribution of resources ranging from immunisation policy in infancy to the provision of care for the elderly or demented. The NHS individual patient requires services for the assessment and diagnosis of his complaint in the context of his pre-existing disabilities; and the safe treatment of his whole case to achieve an optimal outcome. More simply stated, public health resources devoted towards identifying, for example, early diabetes, should not take away from the young mother the medical care she needs for her multiple sclerosis. And even if it were possible to reduce the prevalence of diabetes by publicity and campaigns, the services for individuals with illness from the huge range of uncommon disorders will still be necessary. Both arms of the NHS, public health and individual care, are vital, and they should not compete for resources. The mistake that Lord Beveridge made was to believe that by improving public health, costs of the NHS would come down. Sadly, public health measures will not in the foreseeable future give benefits to individuals suffering from most of the illnesses for which they consult their doctor.

The Public Health side of the NHS must remain political – a government responsibility with the resources allocated as assessed by the government on expert scientific advice. The outcome benefits are usually measurable by statistical means, allowing adjustment of policy as appropriate.

In the last three decades, the Health Service has established a new hierarchy of power. At the top there is direction by Government. At the bottom is the coalface of professional staff and patients. In between is Hospital Management, growing exponentially in numbers and unrelated to any defined need. Hospital Management, like Government, has increasingly cut itself off from being able to judge patient *need*. There are now other determinants of policy: finance, efficiency, use of resources (including human resources), cost benefit analysis (even for treatment, e.g. NICE Committee), and many others. And the Hospital Management personnel are dependent on their ministerial masters for training, career progression, and the direction of policy for the hospital. Patient benefit and medical and nursing care now must be subservient to health care policy directed from the top.

It is surprising therefore that the NHS has worked as well as it has. The reason for this partial success is mainly due to compromise. The politicians have compromised in the face of medical realities – the need to establish costly cardiac surgery or neonatal care units, for instance. And the doctors have compromised by the acceptance of the direction of their services by management and co-operation with marginal policies, such as 'waiting list initiatives'.

But clearly the structure is creaking under the strains of this power hierarchy. The government is blamed unreasonably when anything goes wrong. Patient groups and individuals know that they lack the power to change things (the ballot box surely cannot lead to detailed improvements in the NHS). And doctors have become dependent on management decisions.

The role of the Department of Health should be only to represent the taxpayer and to manage the delivery of services.

The role of the medical profession is to determine standards and best practice and to maintain them in the care of their patients.

The patient is uniquely able to perceive his own needs.

Each point on this triangle is complementary to the other two. If the power relationships can be put in balance each party can fulfil its role to the general good.

Firstly, the Department of Health must withdraw from all areas of personal health care, other than Public Health, overall financing priorities, and the delivery of major capital investments and services (e.g. hospitals, MR scanners and radiotherapy equipment). It continues to have full responsibility for Public Health and for Mandatory Treatment – see below.

Secondly, the medical profession must be given back the power to determine its own standards and to maintain them. This means that Primary Care Services and Hospital Management Services must be managed by a local committee usually under the Chairmanship of a health professional, either a senior doctor or a senior nurse.

The present bureaucracy of quangos has to change from having the power to set targets and direct activity, to a role where it is advisory to the management services who carry responsibility for policy. The NICE committee, for example, would continue to analyse the benefits of new treatment. Its conclusions would be generally available, but the analysis of the cost/ value/ benefit decision would rest with the patient advised by their doctor.

Thus the first principle should be that the patient is empowered to make the decision in his own case, wherever there is a decision to be made. The important issue of Patient Power must be exercised through the doctor at the personal level. But it also needs to be exercised by an independent committee structure at hospital, through regional, up to a national level. It would be this committee structure that took responsibility for executing changes to hospital procedure or facilities at local, regional or national level. Always in these committees, the patient's representative has the strongest voice with the professional and administrative advising within their areas of competence. Professional competence is the perception and maintenance of standards; the administrative competence is financial, and to protect the interests of the taxpayer. This committee structure would be responsible for setting and maintaining standards of practice and the provision of National Health services. The politics of government should not come into it.

Let us turn to considerations of funding and costs. Much of the increased funding of the NHS has been spent on increased pay for the doctors. And this pay increase has been for the same workload; or in the case of General Practice, for workload reduced by an out-of-hours service no longer provided by the general practitioner. But any corresponding improvement in medical services depends upon increasing medical productivity – by freeing the profession from bureaucracy, form-filling, and from management- and target-driven medical services.

Politicians now admit that the new contract was badly negotiated by the Department of Health. The taxpayer and the patients have suffered and continue to do so. Surprisingly, there has been relatively little political repercussion.

The patient is told by the press that much of the funding for the Health Service is wasted and they know, if they are less than sixty years old, that the price they pay for prescriptions is high and unrelated to their ability to pay. This is the only part of Health Service costs known to the average patient. The doctor, especially the hospital doctor, is aware that the cost of treatment for the individual patient is complex owing to a number of interrelated factors. The doctor-patient interface is unavoidable and very expensive. The associated services that are required (x-rays, blood tests, clinics, operating theatres, pharmacy, communication, porterage etc.) are even more expensive. And unlike public health, the outcome measure must be the subjective assessment by the patient. The classical irony: 'the operation was a total success: unfortunately, the patient died,' overstates the importance of asking the patient how successful the operation was.

The distinction between elective and mandatory treatment is of fundamental importance. There is no decision to be made on services where *mandatory* treatment is required such as trauma, emergency treatment and in life-threatening situations. The services to provide the treatment must be so organised that it can be given without delay; and the cost of providing this service must be covered in full by the NHS. However, *elective* treatment, provided at the patient's request, is different. The *value* of elective treatment can only be assessed by the patient: the *cost* must be assessed by the Health Department.

The patient must say what value he places on the elective procedure that he is being offered. What value does this person place on, say, the ten per cent improvement of five-year survival against the discomfort of chemotherapy; or what benefit after knee replacement would he have through being able to walk without pain? Or even – if he could save himself £4,000 instead of a hip operation, which would he choose? These are the decisions that give the patient the *power* to decide whenever there is a decision to be made.

The recent development of a website to collect the opinions of patients on how they rate the treatment they received in hospital is only to be applauded. It allows potential patients to make a more informed choice, as well as allowing the provider to compare his service standards and make informed decisions about how to invest in improvements. But most importantly, this development emphasises that every sane adult is better able to judge his own needs than is anyone else. Thus many individuals decline treatment, when the costs as well as the risks and the side-effects are explained.

If all elective treatment carried some financial cost, this would have a number of effects. The patient would make his judgement of value not only on the expected outcome and risks, but also on the cost to himself as he would when buying his needs in the supermarket.

'Is treatment costing me £5 per week worth it to relieve my migraine headache?'

Or,

'Is it worth a month's wages to have an operation that has 75 per cent likelihood of enabling me to walk without pain?'

Or even,

'If I could save myself £10,000 instead of cancer treatment that has a fifty per cent chance of extending my life by twelve months, which would I choose?'

The danger of this approach is that a population uneducated in the cost of medical and surgical treatment cannot compare value as they can in the supermarket. Even if the cost is subsidised according to the individual's means (unlike prescription charges) the reaction may be: 'I can't afford it.'

But this is a matter of public education and indicates that such policies have to be introduced gradually with the referring General Practitioner advising his patient of the likely value. The doctor would have to explain the risks and outcomes in the context of actual cost.

The 'value' is assessed by the patient: the cost is assessed nationally by the Health Department.

The proposition is that there should be charging for elective treatment according to means. However, not all decisions for *elective* treatment carry the same weight. There is a scale which I will call the 'elective scale', ranging between treatable cancers, at one extreme, where only a minority would refuse treatment and the cost would be largely covered by the NHS; and at the other extreme, cosmetic surgery where the decision was the patient's and the costs were wholly borne by him or his insurance. Joint replacement surgery is elective treatment between these extremes. But the cost of joint replacement surgery is considerable and the 'elective' costs would balance the costs paid by the NHS.

There are other considerations that need to be taken into account when drawing up a scale to represent the patient's perception of need for the treatment contemplated.

As life expectancy increases, the prevalence of age-related disability also increases. But in this elderly population there is also the greater risk of some associated illness and disability. This may compromise the likely outcome from the treatment. The patient's perception of the need for treatment therefore changes with age and this may need to be factored into the 'elective scale'. It cannot be right to give complicated and expensive cardiac surgery, for example, to someone with Alzheimer's disease, unless it is requested and paid for by caring relatives. And joint replacement in a smoker with a history of heart disease or stroke would rate lower on the elective scale than it would in a fit younger individual, and would therefore lead to *greater* cost to the older patient. And finally cosmetic surgery might be indicated for accidental burns, for example, where the point on the elective scale is high, and the State would pay most or all of the costs in contrast to most other cosmetic surgery.

Thus the patient is told the cost of the treatment and the part of this figure that will be due from him according to an 'elective scale', modified by his or her fitness. The final actual cost is reduced, according to income tax bracket (0 per cent for non-taxpayers, 100 per cent for those over the 40 per cent tax bracket). This computation would be simplified and clarified if there was a limited range of treatment costs with, say, ten broad categories; and if the 'elective scale' was also banded into about four or five levels.

One of the most sinister effects of the politicisation of the National Health Service has resulted from management taking decisions which should properly be made by professionals or by the patient himself. In future hospital management should return to an entirely administrative role, with a considerable reduction in numbers and salary costs.

Waiting time targets have distorted priorities when the doctor concerned should have responsibility for deciding the urgency of, say, the removal of a skin lesion (which may be malignant or merely cosmetic). The patient's convenience must be discussed with the doctor, but 'policy' – either hospital policy or still less government policy – should not come into it. Because of the power of choice within the 'elective service' the patient would decide the waiting time he was prepared to accept. Hospital management would be responsible for determining policy.

What would be the benefits of such radical changes?

1. Some of the costs of elective treatment would be borne by what is now seen as private medicine, and would thereby greatly reduce NHS costs.
2. The patient would have the power to act on his judgement of the quality and value of the service offered. This power would drive up standards in a way that the internal market failed to do.
3. The nursing and medical professions would have the responsibility and the power to decide best elective services and to initiate service improvements in response to the scientific advances in medical research, technology and the pharmaceutical industry.
4. Government would retain responsibility for public health services and the mandatory health services, as well as overall provision of hospital investment without being seen to carry the blame for local failure.
5. Some quangos would remain to act as sources of advice to the Executive Hospital, Regional and National Health Committees which would represent patients, professionals, and government, each with clearly defined terms of reference. Chairmanship of these committees would be seen as the pinnacle of achievement for health professionals – doctors in particular.

Index